Endorsemei

In Endurance: 7 Marathons on 7 Continents in 7 Days, Paul Box shares the incredible story of how he achieved this seemingly impossible feat. But more than just a chronicle of his physical accomplishments, this book is also a testament to the power of faith, family, and work. Paul shows us that it is possible to achieve great things, even when we are juggling multiple commitments. He inspires us to believe in ourselves and to never give up on our dreams.

Charles Peyton
Chairman, BMW Dallas Marathon

Paul's writing is not just a memoir of his amazing adventure but a reminder of what it means to persevere through hard things and run with endurance the race God has set out for each of us. Whether that is an actual running race or other sport where we need strength and grit, or showing a light to the world through the way we live and love our families and friends, he gives encouragement through verses, prayers, and funny stories of the ups and downs of running the World Marathon Challenge. I've already shared my favorite quote from this book with my cross-country team and several others: "God made our bodies to move and go and do, and they have more potential than we realize. It's not until we push our minds and bodies to the limits that we realize how much we can accomplish."

Lauren Cavett
Fellow WMC Runner, Wife and Mom of four kids, Cross-Country and Track Coach

Some people make you envious because they seem to have success at whatever they do. Paul Box is successful at whatever he does, but rather than making you envious, he inspires you to higher heights and a better way to live. His story is for the everyday person who knows they are made for more. More adventure. More discipline. More joy. Paul's story of tackling the World Marathon Challenge has inspired me to dig deeper within myself to tackle big dreams and seek greater joy in the process.

Mark Miller
Executive Pastor of Ministries
The Avenue Church, Waxahachie, TX

ENDURANCE:
7 MARATHONS
ON 7 CONTINENTS
IN 7 DAYS

ENDURANCE:
7 MARATHONS
ON 7 CONTINENTS
IN 7 DAYS

A Journey of Faith, Adventure and Self-Discovery

PAUL BOX

XULON PRESS

Xulon Press
555 Winderley Pl, Suite 225
Maitland, FL 32751
407.339.4217
www.xulonpress.com

© 2024 by Paul Box

All rights reserved solely by the author. The author guarantees all contents are original and do not infringe upon the legal rights of any other person or work. No part of this book may be reproduced in any form without the permission of the author.

Due to the changing nature of the Internet, if there are any web addresses, links, or URLs included in this manuscript, these may have been altered and may no longer be accessible. The views and opinions shared in this book belong solely to the author and do not necessarily reflect those of the publisher. The publisher therefore disclaims responsibility for the views or opinions expressed within the work.

Unless otherwise indicated, Scripture quotations taken from the Holy Bible, New International Version (NIV). Copyright © 1973, 1978, 1984, 2011 by Biblica, Inc.™. Used by permission. All rights reserved.

Paperback ISBN-13: 978-1-66289-507-4
eBook ISBN-13: 978-1-66289-508-1

This book is dedicated to the following individuals:

To my wife, Natalie, because you are my other half. Nothing I do is possible without your love, support, and gradual push to help me do more than I ever dreamed possible. I'm more in love with you every day.

To my daughters because I want you to know life is a journey, and God has an amazing adventure waiting for you if you continue to seek him. His beauty is everywhere. He is good.

To my parents because they love me unconditionally and have supported me since playing soccer at the age of three. They never miss any event, even now at the age of forty-two.

To my friend, Matt, because you'll love hearing the running stories.

To my cousin, Matt, because we share life together.

To my fellow WMC runners because I want to tell my story of our epic week. I love you all and can't wait to see you again on a road, path, trail, or ice runway.

To those who have never run a race and may never run a race because I want you to know endurance matters. It impacts who we become. It impacts those we love. It touches every part of our life.

Table of Contents:

Introduction xv
    March 2023 Post-Race Reflection. xv
    Sunday, January 22: Waxahachie. xvi
    Monday, January 23: Waxahachie xxi
    Tuesday, January 24: Waxahachie. xxix

Day 1: Wednesday, January 25: Waxahachie 1

Day 2: Thursday, January 26: Dallas to Doha . . . 9

Day 3: Friday, January 27: Doha to
Cape Town 13

Day 4: Saturday, January 28: Cape Town 20

Day 5: Sunday, January 29: Cape Town 27

Day 6: Monday, January 30: Leaving
Cape Town 32

Day 7: Tuesday, January 31: Novolazarevskaya,
Antarctica 44

Day 8: Wednesday, February 1: Back in
Cape Town 60

Day 9: Thursday, February 2: Undesired
Day Off in Cape Town 70

Day 10: Friday, February 3: Perth, Australia....75

Day 11: Saturday, February 4: Dubai,
United Arab Emirates................ 86

Day 12: Sunday, February 5:
Torrelaguna, Spain.................. 99

Day 13: Monday, February 6, Part 1 of 2:
Fortaleza, Brazil 114

Day 13: Part 2: Fortaleza to Miami 122

Day 14: Tuesday, February 7: Miami,
Florida, USA........................125

Seven Days Later: Waxahachie, Texas 141

Acknowledgments 159

Training Plan...............................162

Schedule 166

Packing List 172

"Therefore, since we are surrounded by such a great cloud of witnesses, let us throw off everything that hinders and the sin that so easily entangles. And let us run with perseverance the race marked out for us, fixing our eyes on Jesus, the pioneer and perfecter of faith. For the joy set before him he endured the cross, scorning its shame, and sat down at the right hand of the throne of God."

—Hebrews 12:1–2 NIV

Introduction

March 2023 Post-Race Reflection
Waxahachie, Texas

A *number of* people have asked me if I planned to write a book about my adventure, so I felt compelled to write something to document the trip. The following pages contain my daily journal entries from January and February 2023 for the days leading up to the race, then each day of the trip is slightly modified only when necessary to create flow. If nothing else, writing this book gives me something to share with those closest to me and is a way I can remember my trip of a lifetime.

I'm not a writer. I'm not even sure if this qualifies as a book. But I am a runner. My hope is to tell the story of my adventure and how God has used running to shape me into his likeness, especially during this adventure of running seven marathons in seven days on seven continents.

This is my story—it is one of adventure, a life-changing week with tales of fifty-mile-per-hour *winds, 90 percent humidity, Kentucky Fried Chicken, and oh so much more. I hope my daughters read this someday and see that adventure is possible. One of my go-to verses in Scripture is Proverbs 16:9: "In their hearts humans plan their course, but the Lord establishes their steps."*

My other hope is that this collection of journal entries inspires others to go run; get outside; find a trail; hike and seek a lifestyle that extends beyond the screens that have become so much a part of our daily lives. The runners I met along this journey are extraordinary people. They are adventure junkies, and I am forever changed by spending a week away with them. They have inspired me, and I hope to share that inspiration with all who read this story of endurance.

Sunday, January 22, 2023
Waxahachie, TX

Oh, have mercy! *The week is finally here. I'm about to leave everything I know. I will board a plane and start my worldwide journey. The World Marathon Challenge is the brainchild of Richard Donovan. It started in 2015 and has been run every year since, except in 2021 and 2022 because of COVID. Since the race's inception, less than 200 people have completed this incredible task (over*

200 after my group crosses the last race's finish line). The goal is to finish seven marathons in seven days on seven different continents. We start the race in Antarctica on Tuesday, January 31, pending any weather delays. If the winds pick up too much or a large snowstorm shifts onto the continent, they may move the race back a day. If all goes as planned, I'll be running eight days from now. Once the first race begins in Antarctica, we have 168 hours to complete all seven marathons.

Richard has warned us to be flexible and discard all our Type A personalities before we get here. Once we arrive, the schedule is simply a guide, but we should expect disruptions. I also need to know there's nothing I can do to fix any issue that comes up. He took care of the previous races' runners, and he'll take care of us too.

Here's the tentative schedule we were given:

Date	Departure	Arrival	Race Info	Est. Time On Continent
1/29/23	no travel		shake out run	all day
1/30/23	no travel		shake out run, Antarctica Race briefing & COVID testing	all day
1/31/23	Cape Town South Africa 9:00 a.m. (5 hr 30 min flight)	Novo, Antarctica 2:30 p.m.	4:00 p.m. start	8 hr 30 min
2/1/23	Novo, Antarctica 12:30 a.m. (5 hr 30 min flight)	Cape Town South Africa 6:00 a.m.	10:00 a.m. start	16 hr 00 min
2/2/23	Cape Town South Africa 10:00 p.m. (evening of 2/1/23) (10 hr 30 min flight)	Perth, Australia 2:30 p.m.	6:00 p.m. start	18 hr 00 min

2/3/23	Perth, Australia 8:30 a.m. (12 hr 20 min flight)	Dubai, United Arab Emirates 4:50 p.m.	8:00 p.m. start	18 hr 00 min
2/4/23	Dubai, United Arab Emirates 10:50 a.m. (8 hr 25 min flight)	Madrid, Spain 3:50 p.m.	6:00 p.m. start	14 hr 00 min
2/5/23	Madrid, Spain 5:50 a.m. (8 hr 20 min flight)	Fortaleza, Brazil 10:15 a.m.	1:00 p.m. start	16 hr 00 min
2/6/23	Fortaleza, Brazil 2:15 a.m. (7 hr 50 min flight)	Miami, USA 8:05 a.m.	11:00 a.m. start	24 hr 55 min

Trip breakdown:

We fly five and a half hours from Cape Town to Novolazarevskaya "Novo" Science base in Antarctica. It's a Russian science base located on the mainland of the Antarctica continent. We should land there about 2:30 p.m. with a 4:00 p.m. race time. The course is a snow-groomed six-loop course close to the runway area.

We will leave Antarctica around 12:30 a.m. and fly back to Cape Town, landing around 6:00 a.m.

From there, we go back to our hotel, the Winchester Mansions, throw our stuff down, and head out to the course located directly across the street. We probably won't have a lot of time to do much at the hotel. By 10:00 a.m. we'll be running the South African coastline in Cape Town for marathon number two.

After Cape Town, hopefully, I will have time to shower in my hotel and grab some food at a nearby restaurant. Then we head back to the airport for a 10:00 p.m. flight to Perth. We should land in Perth at about 2:30 p.m. on February 2. In Australia, we start the run at the Western Australia Marathon Club at approximately 6:00 p.m. This course, like all the others, is a series of loops or out-and-backs. Food should be provided for us afterward.

We leave Perth at 8:30 a.m. on February 3, fly more than twelve hours, and land in Dubai around 4:50 that afternoon. The Asia marathon starts at 8:00 p.m. on Jumeirah Beach. I have no idea what the food plans are for Dubai.

We will leave Dubai at 10:50 a.m. on February 4 and land in Madrid at 3:50 p.m. We start the Europe marathon around 6:00 p.m. on the Jarama Formula 1 course. Food should be provided here also.

We then leave Madrid on February 5 at 5:50 a.m. and fly eight and a half hours to Fortaleza, Brazil. The South America marathon should begin around

1:00 that afternoon. There are restaurants and hotels close by to grab food if there is time.

Finally, we leave Fortaleza around 2:15 a.m. on February 6 and fly eight hours to Miami. We change time zones again and land in Miami about 8:00 a.m. and hope to begin running there about three hours later, around 11:00.

Today's Run::

4.0 miles at a 6:50 pace on the treadmill with some weight training.

Monday, January 23, 2023
Waxahachie, TX

In fifty hours, my flight takes off. It's hard to believe that it's finally going to happen. I started thinking back to how this all started. In 2017, I attended a dinner the night before the Boston Marathon. As I was waiting for my food to be served, Meb Keflezighi and a number of other elite marathoners walked in. Next to him was Kathrine Switzer, the first woman to ever complete the Boston Marathon, and a number of other famous runners. They introduced a young woman, whose name I don't remember, and explained she had *recently completed 7 Marathons in 7 Days on 7 Continents. I was mesmerized. I still am.*

Yes, running fast is awesome, but I would never be fast enough to win a large marathon. That's not a dream worth dreaming for me. I'm not afraid of stretch goals, but throwing down a sub 2:50:00 is a great goal for me (I ran a 2:50:30 at the Boston Marathon on April 17, 2023). Winning anything more than the local small town 10k is a stretch. But 7 Marathons in 7 Days on 7 Continents seemed awesome and possible to achieve. I added it to my internal bucket list.

Fast forward a few years and many races later. I'm trying to decide what my next race will be. I'd run most of the local marathons around the Dallas scene and couldn't decide what state I might want to go visit next for a race. That's when I remembered the girl from the Boston dinner. I researched online and found the World Marathon Challenge. It didn't take much to apply. I found a link, clicked a few buttons, found the outrageous cost, and decided it never hurts to fill out a free application. I was certain I'd never get in.

Weeks passed. I forgot about the application until one day I received an email in my inbox saying that my registration had been accepted. If I was willing to pay three equal crazy payments or one even crazier payment, I could attempt to run the World Marathon Challenge. This was the moment I knew I had to act.

I got home later that evening, enjoyed dinner with my wife and two beautiful daughters, cleaned dishes, worked on homework, and tucked my two girls into bed for the night.

After dinner, I asked Natalie, "Want to go sit on the back porch and have a drink?"

She replied, "Yes, why?" She already knew something was up. I poured a glass of whiskey and hoped she would drink something other than water for what I was about to tell her. I often joke with her and tell her she needs to "have some liquid courage." She usually doesn't laugh. Just gives me a look.

We sat on the back porch. The sun had already set, and a cool breeze greeted us as we sat in our old-person-style rocking chairs. I started telling her about the race and, before I knew it, I told her, "I applied to run this group of races where you run seven marathons over a period of seven days."

She said, "Yeah, I'm not doing it."

"And you do it on seven different continents," I continued.

"What? No." That was Natalie's immediate reaction. I quickly turned into the best possible salesperson I could be. From there, we talked about what an adventure it would be, the ridiculous costs, and more. "Paul, you know how crazy you get training

for a race and how you need to be careful not to neglect your girls. How are you going to train for this and make sure that doesn't happen?"

I didn't have a great answer. All I could tell her was the truth. And the truth was I needed her to hold me accountable. I looked at Natalie, my best friend, and told her, "I won't neglect the girls. I know I can't let that happen. I promise. I won't."

We decided a once-in-a-lifetime adventure like this can't be missed. How could we possibly turn down the opportunity? And with her permission (and her head shaking), the decision was made.

I'd love to say I started training the next day, everything went as planned, and here I am today. But it's been a lot tougher than that. My application was accepted in mid-2021, right in the middle of the COVID pandemic. Originally, I was scheduled to compete in the February 2022 World Marathon Challenge. That race was postponed because of the pandemic. It was rescheduled for October 2022 but again postponed, this time because of logistics. Each of these reschedules was brutal for the body and the mind. I'd start running and training harder than ever before. Then, right as I was gearing up for my final two to three months of training, the race would get moved. I hit rock-bottom mentally in September 2022 after we received word the race wouldn't happen in October. I tried to stay upbeat, but it's hard to stay upbeat when plans fail. I've learned, though, that life is unpredictable. As Stephen King once said, "Life can turn on a dime." I booked a race in Grand Rapids, Michigan. I trained hard, but the race fell flat. I performed poorly. Then I called my old coach, Jeff Ball. Previously, he helped me set my own personal record (PR) in my marathon with a 2:50:11. He helped me complete a one-hundred-mile ultramarathon in under eighteen hours, and he pushed me hard. Throughout my previous training plans with Jeff, I still balanced my time with family, work, and my faith.

I didn't start completely over when I called Jeff. I was in marathon condition in early November 2022, but I wasn't ready for multiple back-to-back marathons. Mentally, I was tired. When Jeff and I started working together again, I had thirteen weeks left to train. Jeff had me focus on multiple long days each week. Most weeks included midweek semi-long runs on Tuesdays and Wednesdays, then long runs again on Saturdays and Sundays. In between these, I would add in shorter mileage on Mondays and Thursdays. Some Fridays, I ran, and sometimes I took off. Overall, I was putting in a lot of miles. Like everyone, life is busy between work, kids' activities, church, and volunteer roles. Some weeks, I would have a rest day, and others, I wouldn't. Sometimes I had to rearrange the training schedule, but seldom *did I skimp on the plan. I stayed disciplined to the mileage. To my plan. To my dream.*

From November to January, my weekly mileage increased from sixty to eighty-two miles weekly with at least six of those weeks above seventy miles. Within the first month of getting back into his training program, I felt my fitness improving. Within two months, I was running strong. Then, I spent a weekend volunteering at the Dallas Marathon. There's just something about being around racers for a weekend watching people compete. Some run fast, others just walk across the finish. My favorite is seeing first-time marathoners finish. There's nothing more awesome than seeing people push their bodies harder than they ever imagined possible! After a weekend of volunteering and two months of hard training, I felt as if I could run through a wall.

Going into January, my body was tired from the training, and at the same time, I felt like I could run for days. Coming off the high of volunteering at the Dallas Marathon, I was ready to increase the intensity even more. On January 13, two and half weeks before our event was to begin, I ran a marathon around my hometown of Waxahachie. I took it easy but ran close to the pace I planned to run for the World Marathon Challenge. I finished in 3:21:24. My body was ready. My mind was ready. Now, it was just a waiting game.

The next day, I was scheduled to run another marathon around the same pace to see how the body would respond. I drove to Irving and ran some nice park trails there with my friend Mark, who opted to ride his bike (I can't blame him). I finished in 3:21:26, only two seconds slower than the day before. This was a huge mental boost. Despite logging over fifty miles in two days, I felt good. I woke up the next morning still feeling good. I was tired, but I could've run again.

The intense training was done. It was time to taper the mileage back and start a little recovery and resting. I felt strong, so Jeff and I decided to not implement too much of a taper since I wasn't dealing with serious injuries. My knees had bone spurs in them (and still do as I write this book). But that was just something I was going to have to learn to deal with. I ran fifty-two miles two weeks out and twenty-eight miles the week heading into the first marathon. (For those interested in my training plan, I've included it at the end of the book.)

Now, I'm sitting here thinking about leaving in two days, and my adrenaline is pumping, which means I probably won't get much sleep tonight. However, before I try to sleep, this is a good time to mention how important it is to have friends who run with you. Running alone has its benefits, but over the months and years, The Waxahachie Running Club and Midlothian Running Club have become a part of me, a part of my family.

Cody, Russell, Maria, Ashlea, Blanca, Virgilio, Taylor, Marty, Julia, Justin, Eric, and so many more are some of my close friends because of time shared pounding pavement. I have two friends I run with more than the rest. Matt Curtis and Mark Miller started as running partners but are now some of my closest friends. Matt and I have run countless races together since 2012 (We don't really keep track of who wins—except for the Hachie 2015). We've run in good times and bad times. There's no one I'd rather have on the road by me. Mark started running with us last year, and his pure athleticism is crazy. He's a beast, and I'm pretty sure he doesn't feel pain. I've really enjoyed lots of spiritual conversations with Mark, and we have had plenty more talks of soccer, economics, politics, family, and more.

I better stop here, or else I'll be dragging in the morning.

Today's Run:

6.11 miles nice and easy. 8:25 pace. Time: 51:26

Tuesday, January 24, 2023
Waxahachie, TX

It's the day before I leave for the World Marathon Challenge, and a million thoughts are going through my mind. For the last two to three weeks, all I've done is think about this race. I wake up with it on my mind. What training do I have today? How does my knee feel? Do I have the right gear? What about visas for each country? And so on ... Then I think or talk with people about the race all day as people call or text with words of encouragement. As the day ends, it's the last thought on my mind as I plan the next day in my head.

I'm anxious. My mind is racing. It's crazy! I'm not so nervous about the actual races. My thoughts race: What if I get COVID and can't go to Antarctica? What if my luggage gets lost? What if the bone spurs in both knees are just too much to handle? What if I tear or pull something and can't finish? Am I neglecting my family for selfish ambitions? Will my daughters see my endurance and perseverance as godly or prideful? How can I use this platform to show others the love of Jesus Christ?

I close my eyes and whisper, "God, please help me with all of this! Here I am, one day from leaving; Lord, please take over. I've laid this at your feet before, only to pick it back up again, but I lay it *down once more, desperately needing more of you and less of me. God, change the rhetoric around this story from my crazy adventure to your child who is saved by grace, pleasing you with the joy of running while sharing your love to the world."* After my prayer, I read Ephesians 2:10: *"For we are God's handiwork, created in Christ Jesus to do good works, which God prepared in advance for us to do."*

Office work is important right now because I leave tomorrow and will be out of town for two weeks, but it's hard to concentrate. My mind is on the ever-nearing task at hand. This is the most epic running adventure in the world. How am I supposed to concentrate on anything else?

For the last eighteen months, I've been training for this event. This hasn't been the only race to train for, but it's definitely on my mind during every race or training run. If I'm being completely honest, it's as though all the years of running have brought me to this point—a culmination of all my effort, pain, and experiences.

My love of running started years ago. I was three years old when I started running with my dad and brother. Our dad would wake us up toward the *end of his run. I'd throw on whatever sports clothes I had, and we'd go outside to run a few miles. My first race was when I was four years old in Dallas, Texas. Every Thanksgiving, my family would wake up early and head into downtown Dallas for the YMCA Turkey Trot. There was a three mile (not a 5k) and an eight-mile option. We usually did the three-mile race early on, but about the time I turned eight years old, we did the eight-mile run. I believe we were just about the very last people to cross the finish line, but I loved it. I looked forward to those Turkey Trot races every year. To no surprise, we kept doing these as a family well into my thirties. Over the years, the race drew so many runners that it would take longer to get across the starting line than it would take for the winner to finish the entire eight-mile race. In lieu of the Dallas Turkey Trot, we decided to run around our town each Thanksgiving. But I still miss the streets of Dallas, the drive to and from the race, time with my family in that electric atmosphere, and the excitement of crossing the finish line.*

The workday is starting to wind down, and I usually leave the office around 4:00 to go for my daily run. But today's thunderstorms will change my plans. I'll visit my local YMCA, jump on the treadmill, and then add in a little weight training.

1987 Dallas YMCA Turkey Trot. 7 years old.

Journal follow-up at 9:30 p.m.

After my training run, I came home to be with the family and put the finishing touches on my packing (which is a story in itself). You want to take everything you might need, but since you'll be on and off planes, you don't want to lug around more than you need. I separate each race into Ziplocs so I can easily grab what's needed before each race. I have one pair of trail shoes, two Hoka Mach 5 road shoes, plus sandals. I also take a number of recovery items such as calf sleeves, my Jawku massager, and more. In addition, I load up a full pharmacy worth of meds. I grab every old pain killer prescription in my cabinet in case my knees cause me trouble. I take blister repair items, antibiotics in case I feel sick, nausea medicine, cough drops, butt paste for chafing issues (trust me, you don't know pain until you've had chaffing), Band-Aids, and even valium to help me relax on the plane if needed. I decided too many meds are better than too little.

Today's Run:

4 miles on the YMCA treadmill. Heavy rain outside. 7:25 overall pace. Felt strong. Need a beer to calm the nerves!

Day 1:

Wednesday January 25, 2023, 3:55 a.m.
Waxahachie, TX

I can't sleep... *It's go day!*

I leave tonight for the World Marathon Challenge, and I'm beyond restless. I've tossed and turned all night and been awake since 3 a.m. That's not good when eight of my next twelve nights will be on a plane. My narcolepsy helps me fall asleep but not stay asleep (Lord, help me rest and get some sleep tonight on the plane).

Before heading out, I make a list of all the things I need to get done today:

- *Eight-mile run at 5 a.m. with Matt and Mark*
- *Drop girls off at school at 7 a.m.*
- *Be at work by 7:45 a.m.*
- *Haircut at 9:00 a.m.*
- *Meetings at the office from 11 a.m. to 3:30 p.m.*
- *Hachie 50 (our annual fifty-mile hometown race) emergency meeting 4:00 p.m.*
- *Pack up, shower, and load everything for the trip*
- *Head out around 6:00 p.m.*

And these are the things I know I need to get done. I'm sure there are other things that I've forgotten. Natalie, Kenlee, and Annie will take me to the airport, and we'll go out to eat as a family. It sinks in. Although it's only going to be a short time, I already miss them a ton! This is going to be hard.

> "Lord, my prayers are many this morning. Please remove the anxiety of all I'm leaving behind at work with the Hachie 50 and more. Help me use this trip to quiet my life before you. Please watch over my family. Keep them healthy and safe. May our distance show each of us how much we love each other. Keep me from getting sick, Lord, and help my legs hold up and stay injury-free. And let my gaze be upon you, take you in, saturate myself in your love, and enjoy your creation. In Jesus's name, amen."

The run this morning was good, but we stopped a little short. I don't figure cutting one to two miles off my training run hurts anything at this point. I dropped the girls off at their school just before 7:00

a.m. and headed to the office. The day started with a frenzy of calls that needed to be returned and emails to answer. From there, I went to see Doyce to get my haircut, which is always fun because we talk about travel and community events.

After that, I raced back to the office for client meetings. Each meeting took a little longer than normal because each person I met with was genuinely interested in my approaching adventure. We talked for ten to fifteen minutes about the races and travel before ever getting down to business.

At 4:00 p.m. we have an emergency Hachie 50 meeting because we learned yesterday our course needed to change for our race coming up in less than three months. I serve as race director with an incredible team for this fun small-town marathon, ultramarathon, and relay race. We make some final decisions about the course, which gives me a lot of peace knowing this is not something I want to worry about for the next two weeks.

I head home, shower, change, load the car, and we head out for our last family dinner together for at least the next two weeks.

Journal follow up 9:00 p.m.
Dallas/Fort Worth International Airport (DFW)

Saying goodbye is never easy. And I'm not sure why this time feels so different. Watching them walk away hurt. Soon, I will be surrounded by a bunch of adventure junkies ready to run the world. But now, as I sit here alone, it hits me ... This adventure will cost me much more than time, money, and pain. It will take me away from what I've known and loved—my family. By now, they are probably already back on the road close to home. My whole world packed in an SUV. And me, well, I'm sitting here in Terminal D.

At least we had one last great family dinner. On the way here, we stopped at the trendy Bishop Arts area of Dallas and found a new Mexican food place. My girls didn't even complain about eating Mexican food this time since they sorta see this as a possible "last meal" with me. We shared our highs and lows of the day and talked about the coming weeks. I wanted to know everything they had coming up so I could add it to my calendar and keep up with their lives.

We laughed and enjoyed being around each other. The tears held off. Until we had our hugs. At that moment, tears rolled down my girls' faces, and *it was wonderful just loving on each other before I said goodbye. Man, I'm gonna miss these three a lot. My girls are great at loving big. But now it's time to start focusing on the task at hand, one that will require every bit of attention, energy, and strength I have.*

I'm a runner. Husband. Father. Christian. Financial Advisor. But running has taken over. I wake up thinking about what run is on the calendar for the day. I go to bed thinking of my schedule for the next day, making sure I know when I'll fit my run in. I'm in a relentless pursuit, running after something, something that, at times, seems so close yet still far away. But the pursuit brings me joy.

Maybe I'm pursuing the next adventure. God has placed a hunger for adventure inside me. Sure, I could go run the Dallas Marathon, one of my favorite races, but I enjoy getting away from the known, using my hobby to explore. I want to push my body beyond normal limits, beyond what most people are willing to do. God made our bodies to move and go and do, and they have more potential than what we realize. It's not until we push our minds and bodies

> God made our bodies to move and go and do, and they have more potential than what we realize. It's not until we push our minds and bodies to the limits that we realize how much we can accomplish.

to the limits that we realize how much we can accomplish.

I want my daughters to see this too. I want them to learn there's more to life than the daily grind. Don't get me wrong. The daily grind is critical. Doing everyday things to the very best of one's ability is what provides the opportunity to pursue extraordinary adventures. It's what drives innovation. New discoveries. I want my daughters to see endurance, perseverance, and struggle. I want them to see the work. The hours of training. The grit. The pain. The joy. The path it takes to do more than what's normal. I want my daughters to aim for more. God didn't create us to just exist. He marked out our paths for us.

If we study characters in the Bible, we see many examples of God providing epic journeys for those who sought after and trusted him. For example, Moses led the Israelites out of Egyptian bondage, sojourned to the wilderness, trekked through the mountains, and after nearly forty years, was able to see his people enter the Promised Land. Likewise, David was an adventurer. He slayed a giant. He didn't back down. Paul embarked on several missionary

> Doing everyday things to the very best of one's ability is what provides the opportunity to pursue extraordinary adventures.

journeys, going from one place to another, telling people about Jesus. He dealt with shipwrecks, prisons, and more. Now that's an adventure. I firmly believe an adventure awaits each of us if we simply search for it and take that first step. And my next step will take place soon.

I'm sitting in the American Airlines lounge at DFW airport, waiting to board a flight to Doha, Qatar. From there, I'll board another plane to Cape Town, South Africa, where I'll finally arrive about thirty hours from now. I'm so grateful for everyone who has helped me get to this point.

Today's Run:

Scheduled for eight miles easy. Shortened to 6.5 because I ran with Matt and Mark, and one of us was short on time. Started with Blanca and Pedro as well. Felt good. 8:28 pace.

Kenlee and Annie dropping me off at DFW airport

Day 2:

Thursday, January 26, 2023
Dallas to Doha

We're flying over eastern Europe right now with about five hours to go before landing in Qatar for a four-hour layover, then on to Cape Town.

I upgraded for this trip. I figured if I'm going to spend more money than what makes sense and am willing to run a stupid long way, I might as well go in comfort. On Qatar Airways, I'm sitting in a Q-Suite. Aside from turn-down service, braised short ribs for dinner, French wine, large screen TV, lie-flat bed, rolling massage chair, pajamas, face lotions, cologne spray, and a swanky bathroom they clean about every ten minutes, it's pretty much the same as flying economy. One other highlight of the Q-Suite is that you can close the door to your "suite" to have ultimate privacy (I wish Natalie was here. I'll get in trouble for writing that.)

Before leaving for this trip, Natalie surprised me with a hardback World Marathon Challenge Devotional filled with letters written to me from some of my closest friends and loved ones. Accompanying each letter were pictures of each person showing some experience or adventure I *shared with them. She told me that she had worked on gathering their words of encouragement over several weeks before having them bound. My plan is to read two or three of these letters every day of my trip. I want to savor the experience and not rush through it.*

The fact that Natalie thought of this idea reminds me how much I love her and how she's always thinking of small ways to show she cares about people. I truly did marry up. I don't want to read it all in one setting, so I started today with the entries written to me from Natalie and my daughters, Annie and Kenlee. I couldn't get through the first paragraph before I was crying like a little baby. Thankfully, the Q-Suite also has tissues.

I'm a crier. I'm not ashamed of that. I believe showing emotion is a good thing. I tear up at the end of almost every marathon. I give Natalie a hard time because if she and I watch a movie together, I'm the one always in tears (which she laughs about). Let's just say we're watching an old WWII movie. The man meets the love of his life, goes off to war, gets put in a POW camp, she believes him to be dead, discovers he's still alive, they finally see each other and live happily ever after. I'd cry. Natalie—not so much. Now, let it be a movie with a dog owner who loves his dog, takes his dog everywhere, and the dog gets sick and finally dies, she'll be uncontrollable. This should tell you where I stand in a house with two dogs.

Plus, I'm okay crying from time to time because my Papa, one of my heroes who fought in WWII, raised a family, and lived faithfully to his Savior, was also a crier. If a person can heroically fight in a war and still cry, then I can too.

Today, God allowed me to enjoy this fourteen-hour flight, sitting alone in my suite, by focusing on him. Jesus often went away to pray. I feel like God is using this trip to force me to get away and pray. I want this trip to be life-changing, not just because of the adventure but because of time with my Lord. I don't want to waste this opportunity! I am also praying that being away from my family makes my heart continue to grow even fonder for them. I love them so much, and about twelve hours after leaving them, I'm missing them already—their laughs and the crazy faces they make.

> "Holy God, how do I ever slumber through my walk with you when you have graciously given me a wife, children, and friends who passionately pursue you? Lord, I love you. I am yours, and you are mine. I feel like this trip could be life-changing, not just because of the running but because I also

need time away with you. I'm nine hours in with five more to go. I need you—all of you I can handle. Father, help my focus be on you even more than the run. Draw me into a deeper relationship with you. In Jesus's name, amen."

Before closing the book, I read the verse she wrote: "Because of the Lord's great love we are not consumed, for his compassions never fail. They are new every morning; great is your faithfulness" (Lam. 3:2–23).

Today's Run:

Hmmm, I've walked up and down the aisle to the bathroom three times and to get coffee once. Pace not recorded.

Day 3:

Friday, January 27, 2023
Doha to Cape Town

We left Qatar after a five-hour layover, and we're about halfway to Cape Town on a ten-hour flight. While typing, Lim, the lead flight attendant on our Qatar flight, walks up and starts reading. She wants to know what I'm writing and asks if I'll include her in my "book." She asks my name so she can buy the book later and hopes I'm a famous writer. She continues to read over my shoulder. I inform her this is my first attempt at writing much of anything, but she was having none of it. She is convinced I'm a world-famous writer, and says she'll buy my book on Amazon. She also gave me her card and asked if I would write a "positive" review about her and the flight on their website. I kindly agree, hoping she'll stop reading over my shoulder. Another long minute passes, and she finally moves on.

I'm reminded of Philippians 3:12-14: "Not that I have already obtained all this, or have already arrived at my goal, but I press on to take hold of that for which Christ Jesus took hold of me. Brothers and sisters, I do not consider myself yet to have taken hold of it. But one thing I do: Forgetting what is behind and straining toward what is ahead, I press on toward the goal to win the prize for which God has called me heavenward in Christ Jesus."

Paul, writing this letter from a Roman prison, was undeterred in his goals. His endurance and stamina are unequaled in the Bible outside of Christ himself and maybe Moses too.

I love to run. "God, help my running be a training ground to strengthen my endurance that allows me to strain toward what is ahead ... to press on 'toward the goal to win the prize for which God has called me ...'" What goal has God called me to win? Currently, I believe it is the following:

1. To love my wife extremely well. To be unified with her as if we were one so that I am worthy enough that she would respect me, love me back, and do life with me.
2. To raise my daughters to love Jesus, obediently follow him, and humbly love others.
3. To love and serve the church. God has placed me in a position to help lead others, and the church needs regular non-minister individuals to guide others.
4. To serve my community through acts of service through my business and through friendships.

> *"Lord, I'm spilling out onto paper what comes to mind as I brainstorm about what is most important in my life. Please, heavenly Father, correct and guide me where my heart can mislead me. Show me what's most important to you and guide me for your name's sake. May my running teach me endurance to press on toward the goal you have prepared in advance for me to do. Amen"* (Phil. 3:14).

I pull up the guide to see what movies are playing. I love good World War II movies. Saving Private Ryan is one of my favorites. Today I chose The Darkest Hour about Winston Churchill during WWII. He had resolve. Nothing could deter his pursuit of victory. His focus never wavered. I need to keep this in mind over the next week because seven marathons on limited sleep and recovery time will be a battle for sure.

I've been flying a total of twenty-three hours so far, and God has used this time to draw my focus to him. Yes, I'm going to race. Yes, I'm here to compete, but I needed these long hours to fix my eyes on the author of my life. I continued reading entries from my

> "May my running teach me endurance to press on toward the goal you have prepared in advance for me to do. Amen" (Phil. 3:14)

friends back home. Today, I read entries from my dad and mom. They didn't even need to write anything in the journal because their life speaks volumes. I follow them as they follow Christ.

Just reading their words continues to help clarify my purpose, my reason for running. It's to "go into all the world," to be a light to a dark world. I have so much more to say about what they wrote, but it'll have to wait as we're about to land! So excited to be there!

After landing, I made my way through the airport, grabbed my luggage, and went through customs. I put the Winchester Mansions Hotel on my Uber app and caught my ride. It was a beautiful forty-five-minute drive through Cape Town. Table Mountain was out my left window, with the Atlantic Ocean out my right. The Winchester was located right across the street from the ocean.

I checked into my room with no real need to unpack since my world is full of travel over the next ten days. And, as much as I wanted to shower, I decided to stretch my legs and go for a run. My training plan called for a shakeout run today, something to get the blood going again after so many hours in flight.

I changed clothes, grabbed my shoes and sunglasses, and then headed downstairs.

The air was a warm eighty-five degrees but really nice. The sun was out with only a few small clouds in the sky. Directly across from the hotel was a field about fifty yards wide where paragliders were landing every few minutes.

I made my way around the paragliders, careful not to get decapitated, and made my way to the wide sidewalk next to the ocean. It was simply beautiful. I took off nice and easy, just stretching out. People were everywhere—walking, jogging, swimming, and playing. I felt so alive.

I ran two miles out in one direction, turned around, and ran back to where I started but decided to keep going. I ran another mile out the other direction and turned back once more to the beginning. Six miles total. That was all I needed, but it felt great to be here. In a few days, I'm sure I'll be running along this same path for my second of seven marathons.

Today's Run:

6 miles along the Western Cape Town coast. I did this after I landed. Beautiful! 7:42 pace. Time 46:17

Cape Town International Airport

The Winchester Hotel in Cape Town with a paraglider in the distance.

Artwork display along the course on my run today

Day 4:

Saturday, January 28, 2023
Cape Town, South Africa

I sat down to enjoy a nice lunch, and the view of the Atlantic Ocean was stunning. About ten miles down the coastline, it connects to the Indian Ocean. I went out earlier for another six-mile run, walked to the grocery store to grab snacks for the flights, and was able to read my Bible for a little bit. Aside from sleeping horribly because of the time change, it's been a good start to the day.

I read Susannah Gill's book, "Running Around the World; How I ran 7 Marathons on 7 Continents in 7 Days", a few months back. She wrote about the importance of bringing extra food on the plane. I brought three dehydrated meals I could eat on the plane. On my morning stroll, I found a local grocery store to purchase peanut butter, crackers, and a box of granola bars.

Yesterday evening, I finally had the chance to meet some of the other runners. We did yoga next to the beach and grabbed dinner afterward. Everyone is friendly and very diverse. Pit is from Luxembourg. Munish is from Canada. Ahmet is from Turkey. Lauren N. is from San Francisco.

Lauren C. and her thirteen-year-old son Carter are the only others from Texas. They plan to run the half marathon version of the World Marathon Challenge. Jill is from DC. Sally is from the UK. Aside from geographic diversity, our running goals are just as diverse.

During dinner, I have a little fun guessing each person's goals for the races. Munish is hilarious. He said he just wants to finish. Jill seems to be competitive in life, but she's comfortable claiming to run slow. Sally dresses up as a fruit or veggie in most of the races she does. She's going as "frozen peas" for Antarctica! I believe Lauren N. is here to compete. And Pit, well ... there's no doubt that he's ready to throw down. It's incredible to hear their stories, listen to previous adventures of climbing Mount Kilimanjaro, running the North Pole Marathon, running the Antarctica Marathon, running the Marathon des Sables across the Moroccan Sahara, and so much more.

These people are not normal. They are incredible! At home, my friends laugh any time I bring up a training run or my next race. Here, it's all we discuss. It's like our own personal Run Camp. And I am reminded of how special this week is going to be. After a brief dinner with these folks, I realize this week is going to change my life, and these people will forever be a part of my journey.

I go into every race with multiple goals, and this will be no different. My "C" goal is to survive and finish. My "B" goal is to average a sub four-hour marathon (sub nine minute/mile pace). My "A" goal is to average a sub 8:00 minute/mile marathon for each race, which is a sub 3:30 average. I truly believe if my legs hold up from injury, the "A" goal is doable.

My coach has spent the last few months focusing my training on this "A" goal. Previously, if I'm training for a single marathon, I have tempo days, track days, slow days, long days, and so on. We mix it up. This training has been altogether different. I have slow days and aerobic days. That's it. On slow days, I'll run an 8:15-8:45 minute/mile pace, nice and easy. I usually do that about twice a week. The rest of the week is working on building my aerobic capacity. Aerobic capacity, aka VO2 max, is the maximum amount of oxygen that you use over time and body weight. It's the idea of using as much oxygen as you can, as efficiently as you can.

As you run, you breathe oxygen into your lungs and blood vessels, where the oxygen is spread amongst your tissues and muscles to be used for your exercise. The more you exercise at appropriate levels, the more efficient your muscles become at using this oxygen.

Five days a week, my training was focused on steady aerobic capacity runs, meaning I would run at the pace I planned to run during all seven marathons and gradually build my VO2 max. I did very little speed work over the last two months, but my goal marathon pace for these seven marathons is between 7:40–7:55 minutes per mile, and I am comfortable running that pace every day for long periods of time.

More importantly, this is really turning into a spiritual journey. Since early December, I have been through tough times spiritually, the toughest of my life. Satan has been on the attack. God is using this time to restore me, give me rest (yes, even while running 183.4 miles), and remind me who he is. I need this time away with him. Similar to needing date nights with my wife, I need to set aside time and get away to be in his presence. It's been a long time since I've done this. I feel his presence and know he is teaching me. And this challenge is teaching me to trust in God more.

> "Lord, I'm very anxious today. My knees hurt. They haven't stopped hurting since November. My calves and Achilles tendons are tighter than ever before, and I'm nervous I'll tear something and not be able to finish. Right now, Lord, I pray from Philippians

4:6–8. Lord, help me not be anxious about anything, but in this and every situation, I'm grateful for your provision and ask for you to keep me healthy. I trust your peace, which is more than I can understand. I ask that your peace, which passes all my understanding, will guard my heart and mind because your Spirit dwells in me. Let my anxious thoughts change to thinking about things that are true, noble, right, pure, lovely, admirable, excellent, and praiseworthy. Lord, I trust you. My faith is in you, Lord. Amen."

Today's Run:

6 miles plus strides at the end. I ran the first 4 at a good pace but still easy; 7:21, 7:06, 7:25 and 7:17. I met Munish on the run, so we ran the last 2 together at 9:52 and 9:39. This was a great "feel good" run.

Finishing my run with Munish

Evening yoga by the ocean

Dinner with new friends. From left to right: myself, Jill Jamieson, Lauren Neuschel, Sally Orange, Pit Van Rijswijck and Munish Mohendroo

Day 5:

Sunday, January 29, 2023
Cape Town

The day started great because I finally had a full night of sleep. My anxiety has been replaced by nerves. There's definitely a difference. I had anxiety about my leg and Achilles' pain, but the Lord has given me a lot of peace. Yes, I still have moments of anxiety about that, but I am here, and I pray I glorify him whatever may come. My nervousness has picked up. T-48 hours! It's getting real. We have a racer meeting this evening. The famous race director, Richard Donovan, showed up last night, and every racer has also arrived. My nerves are crazy!

It's funny how nerves work. Before this week, I've run thirty-five marathons and ten ultramarathons (any distance longer than 26.2 miles). I still get nervous before each one. The nerves are different, depending upon the type of race. If I'm running a shorter race, like a half marathon, I'm nervous because I know the entire race is going to feel like a sprint. The pain is going to come early and stay with me throughout. In a marathon, I'm nervous because I know the pain is coming, but

I don't know if the misery starts at mile thirteen, which is bad, or mile twenty-two, which is great. The longer the pain holds off, the better. The nervousness about this challenge is different because there are so many unknowns. I'm not even sure what I'm nervous about. I'm simply nervous about ... the unknown.

It's a beautiful morning, so I make some time to go visit a local coffee shop in Cape Town. I read a few passages from the Bible and some entries in the journal Natalie gave me. Today, I read a message from my good friend Jason. At just the right time, God placed Jason and his wife Natalie in our lives. With the struggles the first year of marriage can bring, the friendship and godliness of this couple saved us. Natalie and I matured in our marriage, and our love for our heavenly Father deepened because of the community and love of these dear friends.

Community is a word that really hits home now. My family and friends have been praying and continue to pray for me. My running friends have been supporting me, and the love from my work friends is more than I ever imagined. At times, it truly feels like I have a small village of people carrying me on their shoulders. It is amazing to me how I can feel the prayers of others. I've heard others say in the past they could feel the impact of people praying for them, and I feel that now. I feel the prayers for my peace, prayers for my health and safety, and especially prayers that would draw me closer to Christ, while also giving me a chance to shine his light into all the world.

Being in community with others is so important to spiritual survival.

> "Lord, thank you for the friends you have placed in my life. Thank you for the opportunities you have given me to pour into their lives and for their pouring into mine. As your Word says in Proverbs 27:17, "As iron sharpens iron, so one person sharpens another." Lord, I thank you for Jason and Natalie and the witness they are to us and so many others. Thank you for the humble spirit in which they live, serve, and love. Lord, may my life be a light for others as they have been to us. Amen.

After coffee, I come back to the hotel to pass time. A few of my new friends decided to head out of Cape Town for the day to see a few sights, and they let me tag along. It was a fun day of getting away.

Ahmet and his friend, Itan, are from Turkey, and BJ is from Boston. We headed out to Cape Point and Boulders Beach. Cape Point is one of the southernmost points of the African continent. The views are stunning, and the winds coming off the ocean are harsh! We got to see ostriches and other animals in the national reserve. From Cape Point, we drove over to Boulders Beach to see penguins! They were everywhere. I wanted to make sure to get pictures and videos of the penguins for my girls. Being surrounded by beautiful scenery and tranquility today was a nice escape—exactly what I needed. And, in the simplest way, God answered my prayers. I now feel a perfect peace.

We arrived back to the hotel in time for our first race meeting. Of course, we were all excited to kick things off. The room had small flags strung up around the wall, one for each country represented by a racer. I found a seat next to Pit and Munish toward the back. It was unbelievable. I felt like we were about to attend a United Nations meeting or something—except there were more race shirts than suits in the room.

The race director, Richard, walked to the front and welcomed all of us. He was as relaxed and kind as everyone had said, but he was also in control. I felt extremely confident with him in charge. During his speech, he encouraged all of us, most of whom are type A personalities, to relax and not worry about the logistics. He's got it under control, and there's nothing we can do about it anyhow. He handed out our bibs, took pictures, talked about Antarctica, and the travel to be expected between each location. He's got this down like a well-oiled machine. But the one thing that he nor I had planned for was the feeling I started to have.

This was supposed to be the beginning of the single most exciting adventure of my life, but during the meeting, I started to feel a cold coming on. I wanted to hang around and meet as many of the other runners as possible. But when the meeting ended, I went back to my room and crashed.

Today's Run:

I went hiking and found some penguins. I could not leave South Africa without a few penguin pics for my girls. Other than that, I rested the legs today.

Day 6:

Monday, January 30
Leaving Cape Town

I'm one day out and feel like I have a cold. I get tested for COVID this morning, and if it's positive, I'm out. But "I am confident of this, that he who began a good work in me will carry it on to completion until the day of Jesus Christ" (Phil. 1:6). I am confident that God is completing a good work in me, no matter the outcome of a COVID test or a race. I've prayed and asked the Lord for healing. I've voiced what I want to the Lord, but I trust his sovereignty. He is God, and I am not. I will follow him. I pray the prayer Paul prayed in Philippians 1 in my own words: "that my love may abound more and more in knowledge and depth of insight so that I may be able to discern what is best and may be pure and blameless for the day of Christ." Amen.

The morning went by quickly. I got up, had a few minutes to open my Bible, and read. I prayed for my girls back home and for my health. After a brief devotional, I went downstairs for breakfast. Our Antarctica meeting was scheduled to begin around 8:30 a.m., so I went down an hour before to grab some breakfast.

Breakfast has been fun the last few days because I never know who I'll run into. This morning, I saw Jill and joined her. I've enjoyed talking about politics and many other topics the last few days with her. We don't see eye to eye on everything, but we both love our country and running.

We finish our eggs, toast, fruit, and coffee, then head over to the Antarctica logistics meeting, which is to be held right before our COVID testing.

> "Lord, give me strength to run in a few hours after fighting illness and almost no sleep. I am in your hands. Amen."

The COVID testing had me on edge. I still didn't feel good and coming from someone who has had COVID two or three times in the past couple of years, I was not confident in my results. Before the test began, the logistics company went over a few details about Antarctica. The weather was unpredictable, and the weather report we read online was probably wrong. Googling the weather report wasn't easy. And we just learned we can't pee on the course. As a runner, it's not uncommon to see people in long races step off the course a few steps and go if nature calls. However, for this course, we were told we would have to run a good distance off the course if need be.

Overall, we were encouraged to not bring trash or even dirt on our shoes to the continent and do our best to care for the planet. We had to keep it clean. After the meeting, we were ushered outside and then, one by one, were escorted back to take our COVID test. This was a test of faith. I had to trust God that he is good no matter what and that he would be glorified either way. The moment had finally arrived, and they called my name. Although I had prayed and given it to God, I was nervous. The whole trip was coming down to a few colored lines on a test that probably cost less than twenty dollars.

I took the test, had the cotton swab swished around my mouth for what felt like an eternity, answered a few questions for the media group, and I was on my way. I wouldn't have the results of the COVID test for hours.

I couldn't wait that long. I went upstairs, changed into my running gear, and headed out to find a pharmacy. I found one about half a mile away and purchased an at-home COVID test. I ran a little longer, got in about 1.5 miles total, and headed back to the hotel. I hesitated at first.

What if the test comes back positive? I've trained for eighteen months. Shoot! I've trained for twelve years of marathons! I've paid a ridiculous sum of money, and I feel like I have ten thousand people back home following and cheering me on.

I undid the casing around the capsule, removed the swab, and proceeded to jab it into each nostril and swirl it around. I finished the entire test and waited fifteen very long minutes. I walked back into the bathroom where I took the test and looked down. Only one line was showing! Negative! I was COVID-free.

This was great news, but I still felt like crap. I had a cold, allergies—something. I started repacking my gear to take with me to Antarctica; plus, I needed to get ready for the next few days because I wanted to have my gear ready for the following race. Our carry-on luggage was required to have the next race gear in it. This was so we could get ready in the plane if necessary.

About 1:00 p.m., as I was finishing my packing organization, I received a WhatsApp from a group of friends I was quickly becoming close with. Lauren and Munish said, "Richard is bumping up our Antarctica flight. We leave tonight! Meet in the hotel at 8 p.m." A storm was headed toward Antarctica early Wednesday morning, so we needed to get there early, run, and fly out before gale force winds hit the area.

Talk about a shot of adrenaline. We were leaving in seven hours! I took off to get a pizza at a place down the street I had been to a few days before. I ate a Hawaiian pizza and drank a large glass of

Endurance: 7 Marathons on 7 Continents in 7 Days | 35

water. Afterward, I went back to the room and climbed in bed, hoping to crash for a few hours. Unlike the flight out of DFW, this plane ride would not be as pleasant. I dozed off for about fifteen minutes when my phone rang. Natalie was calling. I'm positive there's no better reason to wake up from a necessary nap than to take a call from my bride. She wanted to hear about the Antarctica change and see if I was feeling any better. I was not. But it helped to hear her voice and see her face. I also had a chance to help wake up my girls for school. At 2:15 p.m. my time meant it was 6:15 a.m. back home. Just getting to see my baby girls, talk to them for a few minutes, and hear their voices helped me feel a little better.

We hung up, and I tried to go back to sleep. I should have put my phone on "Do Not Disturb" because I started getting a lot of texts. Words can't describe the amount of support I received for this trip. Daily prayers from the Young family have been so uplifting. One of my friends, Doug, has been sending me daily jokes, mostly involving penguins so far. His most recent joke involved my recent trip to see penguins. He encouraged me to not seek running advice from them due to their "short strides" and "they have a lot of wasted side to side movement! Oh, and tuxedos are not very conducive to running either."

Along with the jokes, my best friend and cousin, Matt, sent some uplifting messages and a few things that are best left unspoken (Ha). One of my best friends, Evan, sent me a note along with many others, and Tyson, a close college friend, is tracking my flights around the world.

To say I am in many people's thoughts and prayers would be an understatement. I have felt enormously loved over the past week, and it's been the most uplifting time that I can remember. It's a little selfish enjoying all of the support. It's also a huge reminder of God's family and how we are to love and support one another.

I never went back to sleep, but I did stay in bed for three to four hours. I got up about 5:00 p.m., showered, and prepared to leave. I decided to eat again before heading to the airport. Munish had told me about a pasta place around the corner. I met a few others there and ate some cheese pizza and spinach ravioli. I returned to the hotel, changed into running tights, and put pants over these for the flight. I threw on a T-shirt, hat, and my Hoka shoes before grabbing my bags.

We gathered on two large buses for the drive to Cape Town International Airport, which was pretty empty at 9:00 at night. We checked into our flight at a desk that had Antarctica lit up over it. This was so cool to see. We all took pictures in front of the sign as they handed our tickets to us. I stopped for another dinner around 9:30 in the airport. I do not recommend Mexican quesadillas from the Cape Town airport, but I ate them anyway.

As we left the terminal, we boarded a bus to commute to the plane. I stood next to David Kilgore as we drove out. He's fully expected to win this week. He's run multiple sub 2:30 marathons, sub 14:30 5k, and is fully sponsored by Red Bull and On. He's here aiming to beat the world record set by Michael Wardian a few years back. He's aiming to average under 2:45 for each race! I'm hoping to see it happen. He is really friendly and seems to genuinely care for everyone else's race just as much as his own.

We got off the bus and looked at the coolest plane I've ever seen. We were flying in an Ilyushin Il-76, which is a Soviet military cargo plane, but ours had been retrofitted with passenger seats. It had windows across the front top and bottom, huge engines, no passenger windows, and on the inside were rows of chairs and what looked like bolted-down bathrooms near the back. I wouldn't want to fly the entire world on this beast, but for a trip to Antarctica and back, it was so cool.

The Ilyushin is very loud. We each got a pair of earplugs, and I fell asleep pretty quickly. After about ninety minutes, I woke up and ate another *dinner. My aches and sickness are starting to ease up. I'm hoping I've just been hungry and that three dinners will give extra nutrients to fight off anything else that comes up.*

It's now 2:13 a.m. Tuesday morning. I need to go back to sleep. We should be landing in about two and a half hours. Man, this plane is loud.

Today's Run:

1.52 miles to the pharmacy. 7:26 average. Total time 11:19.

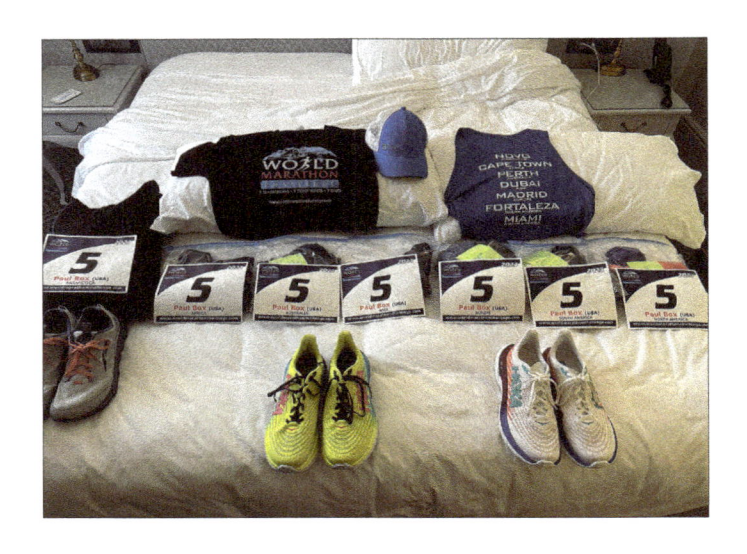

7 packs of gear, 1 pair of trail shoes, 2 pairs of road shoes, RunUnited hat, and 2 WMC shirts

Accepting my bibs at our introductory meeting

Racer briefing on Sunday, January 29, 2023

We all wanted a picture next to the Antarctica sign at the airport.

42 | Endurance: 7 Marathons on 7 Continents in 7 Days

About to board in Cape Town for our flight to Antarctica

Inside of the Ilyushin Il-76 plane to Antarctica

Day 7:

Tuesday, January 31, 2023
Novolazarevskaya, Antarctica

We've been flying *for a little over four hours, and we have a little more than an hour before landing. We are all feeling the adrenaline now. Everyone is getting their gear ready. When we left Cape Town, it was eighty degrees. For the next forty-five minutes, the plane was a frenzy of bathroom runs to change into pants and warm clothes. When we landed, it was eleven below zero, and the wind was blowing a consistent thirty miles an hour with gusts up to fifty miles an hour.*

Covered in a blanket of snow and blue ice, the runway in Antarctica greeted us. The door opened, welcoming in the clean arctic air. It took me a few minutes to exit since I was sitting close to the rear of the plane. As we made our way off the plane and down the stairs, photographers were there to take our pictures. But more than the flash of a camera, the endless miles of pure white snow was my new home—at least for a few hours. The only dirt you could see was on the top of a few small hills in the distance where the snow had been blown off. The cold was a constant companion. The air filled my lungs, chilling me to the core of my being. With every breath, I could feel it deep inside. I quickly realized Antarctica could be unforgiving. There was no escaping the wind's bite. It hit you immediately. The ground was so cold that I could fill the cold coming through my shoes.

We were given two modular buildings to go into where we could warm up and finish preparing about 500 yards from the plane. The ladies took Building C, and the boys got Building B. We were told it would be a little more than an hour to get the course ready, so relax but be prepared. A group of us (David Kilgore, Pit, a few others, and me) made our way to the makeshift cafeteria, which was another building about fifty yards away. Fresh coffee gave a brief respite from the cold. I chatted for a little while before finding a few seconds to FaceTime with my three girls back home. The signal dropped but not before seeing their beautiful faces.

Shortly after 6:30 a.m., we went back to Building B for a briefing. Word came down from Richard that the race needed to start as soon as possible. Winds were not going to improve, and we needed to be done in time to take off before even stronger gale force winds arrived. It was decided the course would be shortened; instead of it being a five-kilometer loop we would run eight times, they shortened it to a four-kilometer loop because of the weather.

The moment had finally come. For the last eighteen months, a year of focused training, and the last six days of waiting, we were about to race.

From top to bottom, I had on a warm Under Armour running beanie with ski goggles. Next, I wore two neck buffers. I had on a tight sports undershirt, a Run United T-shirt, my Dallas Marathon half zip pullover, a Patagonia thin running windbreaker, and my Nike running jacket that I never intended to run in. I wore one pair of Brooks tights plus a pair of Nike shorts, two pairs of long wool socks, and Altra trail shoes. Last, I had on glove liners plus my regular ski gloves. I had on a lot of clothes!

We walked to the start and made sure our GPS watches connected to the satellite, which I was a little nervous about. Runners always want their runs to be documented on some running platform like Strava or Garmin. If it wasn't recorded, it didn't happen. At the starting line, we huddled together for one last briefing. The only warmth was the person next to you. Richard told us they had to shorten the course even more. Instead of loops, we were going to run 1.3 miles out (2.1 kilometers) and back. It was changed to a very short out and back because the winds picked up so much at times that it could've been easy to lose your way and run out into the wilderness where I'm convinced you wouldn't last long. No problem, I thought. Let's just run! It's too cold to sit and talk about it.

Within just a minute or two, we were off. No gun, no horn. Just "GO!" The course was next to the ice runway where we landed. We ran by the plane on each loop. A white plane in a white wilderness. You didn't want to run on the ice because you would probably fall, but you also didn't want to find yourself in four-to-five-inch-deep snow. The winds carried the snow, and our adrenaline carried our spirits. We were finally in pursuit of our first medal. But it wouldn't be without enduring hours of howling wind, slippery ice, and frozen snot.

The winds were at our back for the first 1.3 miles, and you could feel it. It's never great when you can feel the wind at your back because you know when you turn around, it's going to be a struggle. I got to the 1.3 mile turnaround point running side by side with my friend Pit. He looked at me and said, "I'll take the lead for now, and then we'll trade off." Runners and cyclists often do this "drafting" to conserve energy. Running behind wasn't too bad. But as soon as I started to get comfortable, it was my turn to take the lead. I used every muscle in my body to keep going. My abs strained. I had to hunch my back to bend down into the wind. My thighs burned. My calves tightened. My feet dug in, finding traction on the white flakes. My arms *pulled me along. Every muscle was now in motion. And that was only the beginning.*

One loop down, nine more to go. I threw off my outer Nike jacket because I was warm, but other than that, I had the right clothes. Despite my hands being cold, I felt good with what I had on. Pit and I were still running side by side in second and third place. David was already more than a minute or so ahead. We were cruising just under an eight-minute mile. When we ran uphill, we had the wind at our backs. It wasn't a bad uphill. The entire race had 750 feet of elevation gain. The wind pushed us up the hill without much effort ... but the downhill was brutal. We got to the second turnaround, mile 3.9. Pit and I continued our strategy of blocking the wind from each other. Our pace slowed greatly going downhill into the wind. We'd back it down around 8:40–9:00 pace. The winds were a constant obstacle. At times, it felt like we were standing still.

About the time we were finishing our second lap, I started to fall back from Pit. I was pushing hard to keep up with him, but it wasn't worth it. There were still six more marathons over the next week, and I could tell how much this race was going to take out of me. I backed off a little and turned around for the third loop. My pace stayed about the same. I was now running my race instead of worrying about keeping up with someone else. When I turned around and ran into the wind on loop three, I realized I may have made a mistake not staying with Pit. The wind drained me. I still had seven and a half more loops to go, and the mental battle had already begun.

I made it to the bottom of loop three and turned back uphill. By this time, the water bottle I was carrying had frozen, and I couldn't get any water. The only aid station was at the end of each loop. You could run about twenty-five yards off course and jump into one of two tents where they had tables of water and snacks, but it took time and extra energy to do this detour. I held off. Right now, I wanted to finish loops four and five and find myself halfway done.

Loops four and five came and went without much drama. At the halfway point, I was still in third place. David was well in first place, but you could see the struggle on his face. Even for a 2:25:00 marathoner, this was painful! Pit was in second and ahead of me by about a minute. I ran over to the tent to grab two cups of warm(ish) water, drank them quickly, and jumped back out onto the course. Luke Wigman was in fourth, and I wanted to see how far ahead I was. Luke is a very strong runner. He finished the World Marathon Challenge a few years ago in third place overall with an average *marathon time of 3:09. That's really quick for seven straight marathons. I passed Luke about 0.4 miles from the turnaround, so I was 0.8 miles ahead of him. That was good enough for now. Though I wasn't really aiming for a certain place, I'm just competitive. It's hard for me to run a race and not think about where I stand. I was completely happy for Pit and David, and I'd be fine if Luke passed me. I cheered them on when we saw each other and high-fived along the way. (Later in the week, I learned Luke was doing 50ks at each location except Brazil and Miami! Beast!)*

Loops six, seven, and eight didn't speed up, but I was getting through it. On each lap, the loose snow would move from one spot on the path to another because of the wind. It was critical on every lap to determine the best course. You had to determine where the thinnest layer of snow was so you could run there without the additional effort caused by powder or the additional treachery of ice. And, at times, you couldn't see well enough to really know what was snow, ice, or powder.

I made sure to remind myself many times that I was RUNNING A MARATHON IN ANTARCTICA! Yes, it was brutal but amazing, and I was savoring each moment. I remembered an email my friend Russ sent me a week ago to encourage me. He said, "Remember, on every continent, God is there. He laid each stone and built the foundations of the earth." I was running in the most remote area in the world, staring out at thousands of miles of snow and ice and small mountains. These are the works of his hands. I took some time to praise God during these laps, although it was a little hard to praise him heading into the wind.

Loop nine was both great and horrible. Two laps to go. Only about five more miles. I stopped by the food tent one more time (only two stops for the entire race) and grabbed one cup of water and a cookie. I did eat a few gels during the race (I always carry some with me during long races). I started my first gel at mile eight and planned another at thirteen, eighteen, and twenty-two. By the time I got to the gels at thirteen and eighteen, it was a strain to eat them. They were frozen solid, and I chewed my way through them, kinda like a gel ice cream. I didn't attempt the final gel. It would have felt like eating a rock. When I made the turn in the middle of loop nine, the winds were the strongest of the entire day. I had trouble keeping my head up running into the wind as it whipped across my face and stung my cheeks. I tried to smile at the others on the course, but there were no more high fives. We were all in survival mode. I was still in third place, still holding a 0.8-mile lead over Luke. Pit was now about the same ahead of me. David lapped me at the beginning of lap nine, something I would get used to over the coming week. The winds were brutal. It seemed like Antarctica was going to try its hardest to make this 26.2 mile run the most challenging and memorable.

I didn't want to walk because I'd just be out there longer, so I concentrated on keeping up a jog. I looked down and saw I was doing a 10:15 pace. That was fine. I just needed to keep running. We were now facing the strongest winds of the day. It was difficult to make out any sights in front of me to determine how far I was from the end of the lap. I could barely see the plane off in the distance. Pit passed me a few minutes ago as he headed out on his final lap, so I knew I had to be getting close to the end of my lap. I pressed on, looked up, and there was Richard and his crew signaling the end of loop nine.

One more to go.

Loop ten was almost a celebration lap. Yes, I was exhausted and ready to be done. I wasn't going to catch anyone, and no one behind me was going to catch me. I ran uphill with the wind behind me. As I made my last turn, the winds howled but didn't seem as strong as earlier. I ran down the runway track and cheered on others, many of whom still had hours ahead of them in this brutal climate. I loved every second of this final lap. The snow and ice, the winds, the cold, all of it was awesome. I knew I might never get another opportunity like this. I saw Richard at the finish line and could see the World Marathon Challenge banner for each racer to run through. It was awesome! Third place for my Antarctica marathon. My final time was 3:54:42, but I forgot to stop my watch.

Runners stayed on the course for over three more hours. It was harsh. David finished in 3:23:17, almost a full hour behind his personal record (PR). Pit finished in 3:45:24. Everyone was finishing 30 to 60 percent slower than what they would be capable of on a normal day.

I changed clothes but was told no showers were available. After changing and wiping down, I went back to the mess hall for some Russian lamb zopp (this is what Pit told me soup is called in Luxembourgish). It was so good! As I sat there eating and talking with the other runners and even on the plane later, it was hard for me to know how much exertion I put out today, knowing I have another marathon in about twenty hours. We had to push hard today. My body does not hurt, but I'm tired. We ran this race on almost no sleep outside of an hour or two on the plane. We really pushed the limits today. Hopefully, arriving back in Cape Town tonight and getting to sleep in a real bed will give me some needed recovery. One bit of really good news is that my sickness is gone.

We were forced to leave Antarctica a little earlier than desired. The rumor being passed around from some of the runners was that partway into our race, Richard received notice that the Russian Air Force had training exercises planned, and we had to get off their runway by a certain time. I'll probably never know how true this rumor really was, but this forced a few of our last runners to finish their run by actually running directly to the plane from the course as they finished. Crazy!

We took off about twelve hours after arriving. Antarctica was everything I dreamed it would be. None of us wanted to run in perfect forty-degree weather with mild winds. The cold and winds were part of the experience, part of the adventure. The plane ride home seemed to take twice as long as it took to get there. Slightly sore legs stuck into very confined seats made it difficult. Marathon number one was behind us. The journey had begun. It was a great beginning to the most epic running adventure of my life.

A little later in my flight, I reflected on the race. We were still flying back to Cape Town from Antarctica. God's beauty is everywhere. His imagination is incredible, and his creativity is beautiful. How amazing is he!

> "Lord, thank you for so much for today. Thank you for letting me see my wife and girls, if only briefly before my run. Thank you for giving me this opportunity to see a piece of your creation most will never see. Thank you for giving me the strength to get through this first race. Thank you for helping me feel better after having a cold. I know to praise you when times are good but also when they are not. Today was so good, and I thank you for these times. Lord, thank you for giving me opportunities to love and care for others on this trip. Please give me courage to be open about my faith while serving and loving the other runners around me. Amen."

Today's Run:

World Marathon Challenge Day 1 in Antarctica. 26.24 miles at 8:54 pace. 3:54.42. EPIC!

Changing rooms and cafeteria in Antarctica

Antarctica starting line. I'm hidden behind a few people on the right side

Race 1 underway, 3rd from the front

Pit and I finishing loop 1

Endurance: 7 Marathons on 7 Continents in 7 Days | 57

Closing in on the end of lap 2 still with Pit

Crossing the finish line in Antarctica

58 | *Endurance: 7 Marathons on 7 Continents in 7 Days*

Happy to finish in 3rd place

Post-race pic and about to board the flight back to Cape Town. In the background, you can see black poles sticking up out of the ice that marked our course.

Day 8:

Wednesday, February 1, 2023
Back in Cape Town

What a day! *It's 9:00 p.m., and I'm just now able to sit down and put my thoughts to paper.*

Waking up in Cape Town felt pretty cool. I'm ready for marathon number two. My body feels good, and my head is clear. Yes, we're off schedule a little because we left ten hours earlier than expected for Antarctica, but getting back to Cape Town early allowed all of us a night of sleep in a hotel bed versus the airplane which was great. This wasn't part of the original plan, but I'm rested, and right now that's what matters. I woke up at 7:00 a.m., and we were scheduled to meet at 9:30 for a 10:00 race time. I was able to go downstairs and eat breakfast, which I like to do at least two hours before a race. After breakfast, I came back up to my room to get ready. I had plenty of time to read my Bible and read more entries from my devotional book.

I read a message from Uncle Ron and Aunt Donna today. It was about finishing strong, more so as a husband and father, but also in this running adventure. It's a great reminder. Plus, they keep texting to check on me. I always know when it's early morning back home because Uncle Ron will shoot me a text at 4:30 a.m. to check on me. I love it! They have encouraged me in every endeavor. This man fought in Vietnam, ran a tremendous business, and has been someone I've looked up to my entire life. Getting a call or text from him is always a highlight.

The verse that stood out to me in my quiet time was Philippians 1:20: "I eagerly expect and hope that I will in no way be ashamed, but will have sufficient courage so that now as always Christ will be exalted in my body, whether by life or by death." I prayed, "Lord, give me courage on this trip to exalt you in my body and be a light into your world. Amen."

At 9:15 a.m., I grabbed my gear, four gels, a water bottle, shirts for post-race, and headed out. We met downstairs across the street from the hotel. The running path is next to a sea wall blocking the Atlantic Ocean. It was a very warm morning. It was already over seventy degrees and expected to stay in the upper seventies with winds over twenty miles per hour. I gathered with the group outside, took some videos and pictures, and stretched out the tired legs. Such a difference a day makes. Yesterday, and only five hours away, it was twenty-seven below zero with the wind chill, and everyone had on so much clothing you didn't know who was who. Today, it's tank tops, hats, shorts, and shades. I put my AirPods in and turned on my worship playlist. It's pretty easy to enjoy worship music when you're running along the Atlantic and Indian Oceans (very close to where they come together) and staring up at beautiful mountains (Devil's Peak was probably my favorite).

We gathered at the starting line and were off at 10:10 a.m. David took the lead immediately, and within a mile or more, he was out of sight. Another runner, Andrew, from the Cayman Islands, was in second place. My friend Pit and I ran side by side in third and fourth.

This course was six loops, 4.4 miles each along the ocean. We ran two miles out right along the sea wall with the ocean only feet away. Then, we turned back and ran a slightly different trail back that was close to the road on the other side of the grass park. On the way back, we hit headwinds, which worsened as the race went on. Pit and I employed our same strategy as yesterday, taking turns leading each other to block the wind. One of us would take the lead for a quarter mile or more, then we'd switch.

Laps one through three went off smoothly. The volunteers along the course were amazing. They smiled each time we went by and even joked with us a little. Since we ran multiple laps, it's like they became friends as the race progressed. We would smile, say a few words, and tell them we'd see them in about thirty minutes. We also had a fair amount of traffic along the course. People were jogging, walking their dogs, getting ready to kayak, landing from a paragliding adventure, and so much more. Seeing all the people outside was quite the contrast to seeing nothing but snow and ice.

There was a film crew doing some type of video shoot as well, which added to the entertainment. Pit and I guessed they were filming some type of documentary. The security they had for their filming tried to stop us from running through one time, which we ignored and continued on our way.

We were running between a 7:30 and 7:40 pace, and none of the race positions had changed. On loop four, Pit took the lead to block the wind. About 0.25 miles later, we traded off. When he didn't come back in front after half a mile, I knew he was struggling a little. When we made our next turn, I was able to catch a glimpse behind me and noticed he had fallen back about thirty feet. That trend continued for the next loop until I was a good four to five minutes ahead.

I stopped to put on sunscreen before starting the fourth lap. Since I was already soaked in sweat, adding sunscreen just looked like a glob of white mess all across my chest. I'm certain that anyone who saw me enjoyed a good laugh.

I ran loops four and five by myself but enjoyed seeing so many others. It's funny that I really don't know who many of the people were yesterday because of the amount of clothes they had on. Today, it's easier to put names with faces.

As I started my last loop, I noticed I was getting really close to catching Andrew, who was still in second place. I had a cyclist pacing me for much of this race. He looked at me and asked if I was going to push and catch up to second position. I thought about it for a minute but decided pushing to get second place in Africa was not worth it, especially with five races to go. I kept my pace steady throughout and felt good. In the end, I finished third once again. I finished ten minutes ahead of Pit and two minutes behind Andrew. I also finished twenty-five minutes behind David's impressive 2:58 marathon (He ran this 2:58 in heat and more wind only twenty hours after running in outrageous conditions in Antarctica). Overall, I was now in second place with the second-fastest average marathon time, edging out Pit by a few seconds.

After the race, I draped an American flag over me and took some pictures. It felt like I was in the Olympics. I enjoyed time with David, Deirdre, the women's leader, Andrew, and Pit. We celebrated *along the shore and cheered on the other runners as they either finished the race or started out on another lap. It was amazing. This moment had been in the making for several years now, but nothing could have prepared me for the feelings I experienced today.*

Shortly after our finish, Pit and I went to get some food. The best thing about finishing early is having more time to recover and eat. We went to a pasta place about four blocks from our hotel that our group had frequented before. It had quickly become our go-to place. Pit and I went there for lunch and shared a pizza for an appetizer and pasta for our meals. We even had a few beers to celebrate the finish of the second marathon. Pit shared with me that he was being interviewed by the Luxembourg news back home, and immediately, the joke became that I was "Luxembourg famous" because in many of his pictures, I was running with him or drinking a beer with him. About four hours later, we went back to the same pasta place with a larger group and ate the same again. I've always heard that running an ultramarathon is an eating contest with some running mixed in. If you stop adding calories, you can't finish strong. I know I can't quit eating this week.

We received word that our Australia flight was being delayed, something to do with needing a signature from the African authorities. We would have to stay in Cape Town another night and well into tomorrow. We didn't know what this meant for the rest of the week but believed we would need to squeeze a few marathons in with very little rest at some point. I need to take advantage of getting to sleep one more night in an actual bed.

Two marathons down! I'm receiving unbelievable support from friends and family and even strangers back home. Now, I need to focus on staying healthy (there's a stomach bug going around the runners) and keeping my legs cared for.

(Over the next week, more than half of the group got a stomach bug. Dr. Dave gave out so much Imodium and other medications and IVs that he had to get more. Jill actually threw up on all seven continents during seven marathons over seven days.).

Today's Run:

World Marathon Challenge Day 2 in Cape Town, South Africa. 26.58 miles at 7:36 pace. 3:23:44. Really warm and windy. 20+ mph winds with temps over 80 degrees.

Pre-race in Cape Town: Munish, Pit, Lauren, and myself

Marathon 2 starting line in Cape Town

Lap 2 with Pit along the sea wall

Marathon 2 finish

Finish of Marathon 2 and feeling patriotic

Day 9:

Thursday, February 2, 2023
Undesired Day Off in Cape Town

This was an unexpected and undesired day off. Yes, it's nice to have an extra night in a normal bed, but I came to run, and I'm itching to get back out there. From a logistics standpoint, we have seven days (168 hours) to complete all seven marathons. The clock started ticking as soon as the first marathon started in Antarctica. And the last thing I want is to not meet the time cutoff due to logistics.

The problem is that we left for Antarctica nine to ten hours earlier than expected because of weather. Then we ran Africa but couldn't leave for Australia. We were supposed to leave for Australia twenty-four hours ago. Therefore, we lost nine hours in Antarctica plus twenty-four hours in Africa. That's thirty-three hours behind schedule. The race had banked us extra time in Miami. The original plan was to get to Miami and have twenty-five hours to run. Subtract the thirty-three hours we've lost, and we now get to Miami eight hours past our deadline.

We were told several different things are happening to make up some of that time. First, Richard hired a different flight crew for almost every flight.

This will keep us from needing to wait a necessary amount of rest time for each crew on each continent. Also, we don't know where we will run in Spain. Originally, the plan was to run on the Jarama Formula 1 course in Madrid, but we were told we might have to run much closer to the airport.

There are good and bad parts to all of this. First, I feel very rested. I didn't have to run a marathon today, and my body feels so much better than it felt when I woke up this morning. The bad is that we are all itching to run! We've joked about just letting us get off the plane at each airport, run laps around the plane, and then get back on. Let me tell you, these people are running junkies! Another negative is that as much rest as we've been given after the first two marathons, we'll be running five marathons in four days to finish. And from Dubai all the way to Miami, the schedule gets tight, and there will be a lot of running with minimal rest.

My new really good friends, Pit and Munish, and I went out to eat at a beautiful place overlooking the ocean. We had burgers, fries, pizza, and beer. We're taking in as many calories as possible. My coach, Jeff Ball, keeps pushing me to eat a lot and drink as much as I can, although I'm certain he wasn't speaking of beer.

Around 7:00 p.m., we all met downstairs at the hotel to board buses for the airport. I'm finally *saying goodbye to Cape Town, which has become my home away from home. We never intended to stay quite this long.*

We made our way to the airport, went through customs and security, and made our way to our new home in the sky. This plane would be where we spend the next five days. It was a normal-looking American Airlines type of plane (although it was a few years past its prime—it even had ashtrays). There were business class seats that laid down almost perfectly flat, premium economy, and economy. Each day, Richard would email the group to let us know where we'd be flying, and he rotated us between seats.

After a brief screening in customs, we boarded the plane and finally took off. We were on our way to Perth, Australia. The pilot said we'd arrive by 2:15 tomorrow afternoon. Hopefully, they'll bring some dinner soon, and then I'll go down for the night.

On a totally different note, I've continued to read the devotional book. Today, I read a message from Adam, who has become a very good friend over the past two years. He is exactly what I think of when I consider the verse "As iron sharpens iron, so one person sharpens another" (Prov. 27:17). I watch the way he runs his business, cares for his community, and loves his family. It's inspiring. At the same time, he writes a message to me with encouragement and kindness of how I've been able to encourage him. It is such a blessing to be in community with other men who want something more than what this world has to offer. I'm talking about men who desire to love others by serving people sacrificially. I'm talking about people who want to live out verses like the one in Hebrews 12:1, which states, "Throw off everything that hinders and the sin that so easily entangles. And let us run with perseverance the race marked out for us". I'm extremely grateful for a handful of friends that God has placed in my life.

And I'm grateful for the new friends on this trip. I've enjoyed time with Amy, a mother of three from Iowa, sitting next to me on the plane. I had a great day hanging out with Munish and Pit. People like Sally just make me laugh. It is incredibly fun to adventure with this group. No one is better than the other. It feels like we are all on a journey together, one team, pulling for each other. I'm really ready to run, but it's been a good day.

Today's Run:

Nothing. Nothing at all. And it felt good.

Unexpected day off lunch with Pit and Munish outside of Cape Town

74 | *Endurance: 7 Marathons on 7 Continents in 7 Days*

Day 10:

Friday, February 3, 2023
Perth, Australia

We just finished running Australia. I'm exhausted. I wish I wasn't this tired after marathon number three, but the ninety-five-degree temperature combined with travel made today tough.

It's been a circus. This is just a rumor floating amongst the group, but we found out today that our group had to bribe a lady in charge of travel in the Cape Town government for our plane to leave yesterday. First, my friend Ahmet had to contact his close friend, who is a Turkish ambassador in Vietnam, to make some contacts in South Africa to get things moving, so, hopefully, we'd be able to leave the country. The rumor is that the lead of the government travel office wanted a bribe. And what bribe did she want? KFC. Yes, Kentucky Fried Chicken for her entire office! Kinda makes you wonder what will happen next. And it's amazing that fried chicken is what got us up in the air.

The race went well. It was twelve loops of approximately 2.2 miles, or something close to that. Pit and I ran the first six miles or so together. My plan was to start close to an 8:00 pace then get *faster every three laps. My hope was to run the first quarter close to an eight minute/mile pace, the next quarter close to a 7:45 pace, and continue to gradually pick up the pace. I wanted to negative split the race (a negative split is when you run the second half of the race faster than the first half). It's a tough strategy, which only happens when you run smart. I succeeded at my plan, but I'm not sure what it may cost me going forward.*

For the first three laps, the temp hovered around ninety to ninety-five degrees, so starting off slow was an important strategy. I am grateful I thought through this race ahead of time. By the time I got to loop four, the sun was setting, and the Perth running trail really came to life. People were rollerblading, zip lining, jogging, walking, dancing, and more all along the course. There was a huge stadium, which I'm guessing is for rugby or Aussie rules football. There was also a large cricket stadium across the river. It was a lot of fun running next to all the excitement.

Pit and I took off together like we had in every race so far. The course was on soft track material and easy to run on. We ran out one direction for almost a mile, turned around, ran back through the start/finish area, and did another out and back in the other direction. Pit and I stayed side-by-side for about the first six laps.

I continued to pick up the pace on laps seven to nine, and Pit was no longer with me. Coming from Luxembourg, he's definitely not used to ninety to ninety-five-degree weather. This guy can run, but if there's anything that might possibly slow him down, it's the heat. Some of the runners were starting to struggle due to the temps. It can be good to train in Texas. The heat was just tough tonight. The only blessing was the low humidity.

I started pushing the pace on my last five miles and even ran the last four at a sub 7:30 pace. The air was cooler as nighttime set in. I came across the line in third place again, with an overall time of 3:24:50, only about a minute slower than Cape Town.

I hope I didn't over push it today. I still have a lot of running left to do and can't afford to be spent right now. Pit finished fourth while my other good friend, Munish, finished further back, but he doesn't care. He's just having a blast. David finished first, somewhere around 2:50:00, I believe. Andrew finished second in Africa and again here. I lead him overall because of my Antarctica race time, but he's gradually catching up.

After the race, the Western Australia Marathon Club served up the best barbecue we could ask for. They cooked tons of ham and eggs on a griddle outside, served up on buns with barbeque sauce. It was amazing! They ordered pizzas and other great food. Pit and I grabbed a few beers each and enjoyed the evening. Other runners would continue running for a few hours, so we had time to kill before heading to the airport. This was the one time our flight crew wouldn't change. By 3:00 a.m., Jill had a big group of us doing yoga on the outside lawn next to the beautiful skyline and river. Yes—3 a.m. yoga is a first for me. Pit and I made it "Beer Yoga."

The plane trip last night helped. I sat in business class and slept a good six hours before landing in Perth. Tonight, I'm in premium economy. From what I hear, that means I need to actually find a row in economy and claim the entire row for myself to lay out and sleep. Richard gave each of us a small portable air mattress to use on the plane. The plan is to stake out an entire row for myself, put the air mattress on the ground in the row, and after takeoff, hunker down to sleep. I definitely need some rest after today. I really hope to go into Dubai feeling as rested as possible.

It's now 7:00 a.m. in Perth, and we've boarded the plane and are just waiting to take off for Dubai. I feel better than I did right after I finished. I'm tired.

No, that's not true. I'm exhausted, but I still have gas left in the tank. There are four more races in a tight window. Time to suck it up. Even though it's 7:00 a.m., time no longer means anything to us. We sleep when we get on the plane. Other than that, we run and eat.

I did find an entire row in economy and aired up my thin air mattress across the floor. Pit's a row in front of me. Munish is right behind me. Let's hope the air mattress provides enough comfort to sleep for a while. I need rest! We all need rest.

Spiritually, it was a good day, but nothing stood out. I don't want to let exhaustion get in the way of my witness or keep me from serving and loving others on the trip. Instead, I want to be a light that draws people to Christ. "Lord, give me rest, I pray, and help me live tomorrow for you in such a way that others see my works but look to you. Amen."

Today's Run:

World Marathon Challenge Day 3 in Perth, Australia. 26.50 in 3:24:50 for a 7:42 pace. Hot!

Sitting in business class next to Amy leaving Cape Town. David is behind me, probably the only time he was behind me the entire trip.

Our home in the sky for five days

The start of the World Marathon Challenge Race 3 in Perth, Australia

Running next to Optus Stadium

My friend Ahmet Uysal pushing hard and having fun in Perth

Lauren Cavett enjoying the adventure in Perth

BJ Williams handling the heat

Munish always having fun

Pit and I running next to the Swan River in Perth

Evening setting in Perth along the Swan River

Finish Australia in 3rd place; 3:24:50 in intense heat

Day 11:

Saturday, February 4, 2023
Dubai, United Arab Emirates

We landed in Dubai earlier today. I've now lost track of time, days, continents, and everything else, so I have no idea really when we landed. The good news is that I slept awesome last night on my air mattress. I got a full nine hours, woke up in time to eat breakfast, and started changing into my Asia running gear. After changing, I had time to read my devotional book. This time, I read entries from my good friends Stanley and Patrick. These men are "Doers." They love to be the hands and feet of God, and they're inspiring.

I also texted back and forth with my brother, and he's not one to be "touchy-feely." But he put his heart into his texts on this occasion. He's really been praying for me and believing God is doing something special, especially today here in Dubai. He's checked on me numerous times, and it's been fun connecting with him throughout this trip.

My coach, Jeff, and I talked yesterday and planned to start the Dubai Asia marathon running a smart 7:50–8:00 pace and keep that for a while. The plan was to see what the legs have left in them since Australia took so much out of me. Jeff's training has never let me down, and I fully trust his expertise.

Outside of running, I continue to receive amazing support. Of course, my wife has been my biggest fan. Every day while we FaceTime each other, she takes random pictures of me, posts them on FB, and later writes a little text about what each picture is about. It's actually hilarious as she replays our conversations. No doubt people are enjoying her updates on FB more than mine, which is nice because it takes the pressure off me to write out a special race message each day. She is amazing and genuinely cares about what I'm doing. But I also have so many others texting, emailing, calling, and using social media to reach out. It's inspiring. And I know people back home want this adventure to go well for me. It's starting to really hit me—I now represent more than just myself on this trip. I'm representing my family, my community, and my Lord.

After we landed, we made our way through customs and grabbed our luggage. We boarded two buses to drive to the Jumeirah Beach along the Persian Gulf in the heart of Dubai. The city is clean and beautiful, yet three million people call it home. We passed Lamborghinis, Rolls Royces, and so many other luxury cars. This UAE city definitely attracts some of the wealthiest people in the world. But the luxury of Dubai would be short-lived for me and the runners. We were here for business.

The buses stopped by the beach at a hotel where we unloaded our luggage, but the race was already running behind schedule. We quickly left our bags on the sidewalk for others to take inside. Richard pushed us to get to the starting area. The start/finish line arch and the rest stop weren't even set up yet. Richard said they'd get the water stop set up during our first out and back.

Richard shortened our racecourse since we were running in the middle of the afternoon/evening instead of the middle of the night as originally planned. There were tons of people out at this time of day. It was easier to keep track of everyone with the course shortened. He made it a 1k out and back (2k total for each loop, which meant a total of 21 loops, plus a little extra in the beginning to equal 42.2 kilometers or 26.2 miles. Some people hate multiple loops (or out and backs), but I enjoy them. It's fun passing each runner and encouraging each other throughout the course of the race.

The course was run along the beach, and half of the path was a rubbery material, which made for less stress on the legs and feet. The other half of the path was a boardwalk style with wooden boards. I stayed on the rubbery path side because my knees enjoyed the softer landing. I'm so glad we didn't have to run on sand.

The weather was perfect running weather—mid-sixties with low humidity. It's still hard to fathom how weather patterns and conditions are so different across the world. The beautiful weather made for a great day for many people to come out. Individuals, kids, and families were scattered along the beach. Families played in the sand, and young people hung out along the pathway. It was the perfect evening to spend outdoors in this beautiful city. We dodged walkers, other runners, people coming and going from the beach, families, and even people who looked as if they were walking home from work. The beach must have been 100–200 yards wide and miles long. Kite surfers were out in the water, and people were doing a number of other fun activities. It was fun watching them as we got started. But hands down, the best view on this run would have to be the Burj Khalifa, the world's tallest building standing over 2,700 feet tall. It was well off in the distance but awesome to see.

I followed Coach Jeff's advice and kept my early miles between 7:50–8:00. Pit, my normal running partner, took off at a faster pace, and for the first time, we didn't run together. I did get a new running partner for about eight miles. Thirteen-year-old Carter joined me. He and his mom, Lauren, are the only other Texans on the trip; they're from Beaumont. It's awesome watching a young teenager attempt this challenge. He's running the half marathon version of the challenge, but it's still awesome! Today, he wanted to run his fastest time ever (which he did by over two minutes).

I had planned on listening to worship music during the race, but while my AirPods showed they were charged, they had zero battery. I stuffed my phone in my carrier and played the music out loud. It was nice worshiping as I ran. When I back off the pace a little, it helps me pray more and spend more time thinking about my Savior. While running, I heard the prayer sirens go off in the evening, reminding me that all people, no matter what country or what faith, have more in common than it may seem. As I ran, I listened to worship music and praised God for his creation.

And then I started thinking about how much I miss my family. I'm really ready to see them. I'm tired, exhausted, but I can't believe this experience is nearing the end. "Lord, help me finish strong in my running, but help me more to be your witness for others to see. Jesus, be with me in a way that you're constantly on my mind. Amen."

Around mile eight, Carter and I split apart. At mile ten, I started running a 7:40–7:45 pace. I was in fourth place behind David, Andrew (who has *finished second the last two races), and Pit. It didn't look like I would catch any of those guys. They were cruising along, and there wasn't enough time and distance to make up any ground. The short loops helped the time pass because it felt like you were turning around and going the other way every few minutes. Somewhere along the course, you stopped cheering as much for the other runners, not because of exhaustion or negativity, but because you saw them so many times, and saying the same "looking good," "stay strong," "have fun," or something else just got old. I usually gave a thumbs up or hang loose sign and went on my way.*

At twenty miles into the race, I still felt good. I can say that four marathons into the week, my body is tired. But today, I'm simply tired of running. It does get old after three and a half hours of doing the same thing every day. I kept plodding along, lap after lap, high-fiving other runners, yelling random, encouraging words along the way, and enjoying the presence of so many new friends.

The race ended. I came in fourth with a time of 3:25:17, only one minute slower than Australia, where I put out way more effort in the heat. And I was only two minutes slower than Africa, where the wind made it tougher. I felt good after this race! I really hope that translates into a good day tomorrow because we have three marathons to complete in the next thirty-six hours. We will run in Madrid in the morning, supposedly around 8:15, which probably means closer to 10 a.m. Then we jump back on the plane for Brazil to run tomorrow night.

After the Dubai race, we have a four-bedroom condo close to the beach so we can shower and repack any luggage. We repack after every race to put anything in our carry-on we will need for the next day. All of us crammed into the condo, got in lines for showers, and spread our luggage across the floor to repack. We had pizza, cakes, water, and a few other items available to us. We headed back to the airport, and I grabbed more food in the terminal. And as soon as I grabbed my food, it was time to head toward the gate—Dubai was a quick turnaround. Almost everyone has boarded the plane except me and a few others, so I'm signing off.

Today's Run:

Dubai Asia World Marathon Challenge Day 4 Marathon 26.51 miles in 3:25:17. Feel good. Nice and easy.

My economy sleeping conditions from Perth to Dubai

Good friends Chris Yanney and David Kilgore on Jumeirah Beach in Dubai

Pre-race in Dubai

Dubai starting line

Along the course in Dubai

96 | *Endurance: 7 Marathons on 7 Continents in 7 Days*

Carter and I on the course running along Jumeirah Beach with the beautiful Burj Al Arab in the background

Early miles in Dubai

Nighttime in Dubai

Day 12:

Sunday, February 5, 2023
Torrelaguna, Spain

I'm getting close to landing in Madrid for the European leg of the journey. I slept pretty good again last night, but better than that, I woke up to read my devotional book. This morning, I took time to read four entries from Drue, Zach, Mark, and Matt C.

Drue encouraged me to focus on God's unfailing love and he is one of the most loving and caring people I know. He is a servant. Zach talked about training for holiness to become more like Christ. Zach is a leader who is also in pursuit of more of God. He wrote about God's unfailing love and striving to be holy as God is holy. These words were so refreshing.

Mark and Matt know me better than most, but more than that, they know what I need to hear while running. Mark reminded me that God is my strength, and in all likelihood, I'm getting stronger as this journey continues. The word "stronger" really stuck with me. Matt encouraged and lifted me up as he has done for more than eleven years of running together by telling me I'm stronger than *ever and that he's here with me in spirit. Plus, it wouldn't be Matt without a little joke at each other's expense. I really don't think I'd be here without the support from Matt and Mark.*

"Lord, these men make me strive to be a better man, husband, father, boss, advisor, Christian, and runner. Bless them, Jesus, I pray, and help me be for them what they are to me. Amen."

We landed in Madrid about 10:00 a.m. Honestly, the time, days, even the continents, are all a blur. The race was supposed to begin at 8:15 a.m., which won't happen. It does help that we were told yesterday to put everything we would need for Spain and Brazil in our carry-on luggage because we won't have time to wait on bags to get off the plane. We are doing our best to make up time, which doesn't seem to be happening easily.

We stepped off the plane, made our way through the large airport, and we all had to load up onto one bus instead of the customary two. Only one bus is needed now since we have significantly fewer bags.

We took an hour drive to Torrelaguna, Spain. The course was originally scheduled to be at the Jarama Formula 1 racing course, but we needed to find a new location because we're a day behind, and the Formula 1 course had another event going on today. This is a pretty small village outside of Madrid, and a lot of the town's residents came out to cheer us on. The mayor was there to welcome us, give us goodie bags, and kick-off the race. This town reminds me of the small-town feel you get in the Texas Hill Country with great people and a cool vibe.

We met at a small sports complex that had a practice soccer field and locker rooms with showers. Everyone jammed into the building, tossed our bags into the locker room, lathered up with Vaseline or some other anti-chafing cream, and found some snacks they prepared for us.

Two days earlier, or sometime in the last few days (again, time is a blur right now), Pit's wife, Laurence, reached out to me via Facebook. She was flying into Madrid from Luxembourg to surprise Pit and watch him run. Her schedule had been thrown off because we were running a day late, plus our plans changed. We were no longer planning to run in Madrid. She was hoping I would be able to help Pit get off the plane quickly and to the starting area so she could see him. The problem is that we learned we have no control over how fast we get anywhere. We realized we were at the mercy of the airports, buses, and more. We continued to message back and forth as we landed and started moving toward Torrelaguna. Once we arrived, it took us another thirty or more minutes to throw our stuff down, grab a snack, and gather everyone together.

The course would start in the city square next to a beautiful Catholic church surrounded by little shops, bars, and restaurants on cobblestone streets. To get to the city center, we all met outside the sports complex and walked approximately half a mile together. All this time, Laurence was waiting for Pit to get to the starting line to see him.

Finally, we walked into the square, which was surrounded by old, beautiful buildings. It was like I had set foot on the set of a Hallmark movie when Pit saw his wife. There was lots of laughter and probably a few tears. Laurence, Pit's sister, mother, and another friend all came to watch him run. They were so much fun! We've been working on making Pit Waxahachie famous because he's all over my Facebook page. Since I was becoming "Luxembourg famous," turnabout is fair play. Thanks to Natalie's Facebook posts, pictures of Pit and me together during the races, and her FaceTime videos, he had officially been "adopted" by many of my Waxahachie friends and family. No doubt I want to make a trip to Luxembourg someday. I enjoyed meeting his family, taking a few pictures with them, and learning a few Luxembourgish words.

All of the racers took ten to fifteen minutes to enjoy the atmosphere in this small square. One of *our runners, Michael, was dressed up as a bull to run this marathon, and someone found a red flag. We took pictures as Michael ran toward the flag. For a brief moment, we were no longer runners. We were spectators watching a matador in a bullfight. We laughed so hard.*

On a side note—Michael dressed up on every continent, which was fun to watch. I still can't comprehend how he managed to pack everything.

Here's a quick rundown of his costumes:

- Antarctica: a penguin
- Africa: a zebra
- Australia: a kangaroo
- Asia: a panda bear
- Europe: a bull
- South America: a tropical bird
- North America: an alligator

After everyone took pictures and finished soaking up the atmosphere, it was time to start the race. We ran from the town center through the narrow cobblestone streets, passing bakeries and shops as we made our way onto a small road next to the soccer and sports complex. The main course was approximately a 1k loop on roads close to the complex. It was extremely hilly. In fact, the town of Torrelaguna sits at an elevation of 2,400 feet, which is not a lot, but when you've been running at sea level for four straight days, the small amount of elevation can be felt. Plus, the entire course was on a hill, always running up or down. My Strava activity showed I had 1,624 feet in elevation gain during the course compared to only 102 feet of elevation gain in Dubai.

The majority of the climbing was done on two steep climbs, but the whole loop was a hill. The main decline was steep enough that most of the time, we would drop down to low six-minute miles or even high five-minute miles just for a hundred yards or so. Sounds fun, but the steep declines definitely work the quads. For the first time this week, the bone spurs in my knees were hurting pretty bad.

Although my knee pain intensified as the race went on, I felt good from yesterday. I had run a smart race in Dubai and prepared myself to run again. Today, I felt different. I felt like going for it. I was a little tired of running smart for the four previous races. I wanted to push a little. Pit asked me in the beginning if I was planning to run with him, and I said, "I will for as long as possible." When the race started, David took off, but Andrew, Pit, and I filed in together.

The last three races, Andrew has finished in second place and has taken off very fast to fade *toward the end. He's got a lot of speed but has had trouble holding it the last few races. When it comes to rankings so far in the World Marathon Challenge, I'm still ahead of Andrew because he was slower in Antarctica by almost twenty-seven minutes. However, he's finished two minutes, five minutes, and ten minutes ahead of me the last three races, so it's getting close. But I'm still about ten minutes ahead of him overall. After Pit finished five minutes ahead of me yesterday, he's taken back over the second overall position and leads me by about two minutes. Dave is in first by a long shot. He would need to break two legs and maybe a hip for us to catch him. It's actually nice having Dave here because there's no pressure on trying to push and win. There's no way we can catch him. He's a professional and simply faster than we are. As much as I'm enjoying going for second or trying to stay in third, it really doesn't matter. I like the competition aspect, but I'm not going to beat myself up if I end up finishing behind the others. These are great guys and fun to run with.*

Together, the three of us leave the cobblestone streets around the city square and start the thirty-two laps around the sports complex. From the beginning, we were moving much faster than any race so far, and this was marathon number five on a hilly course. The weather was nice, although slightly warmer than we would have wished. At the start it was about fifty-five but warmed up to the mid-sixties.

The first eleven miles were between 7:04 and 7:15 pace. We were running at a good clip. Miles twelve and thirteen were in the 7:20 range but still strong. We came through the half marathon mark moving well. Andrew, Pit, and I were still together.

For miles fourteen to twenty, we averaged a 7:15 pace, but by mile sixteen, Andrew started to slowly fade back from us. I thought I was fading back, but the miles kept clicking by. Every time Pit would put a step on me, I caught him on the next up or downhill. We were step for step.

Miles twenty-one to twenty-six were tough but fun (the most fun I've had all week). Pit and I continued to run together. I don't think either of us wanted to strain to push away from the other. We still had two more marathons to run over the next thirty hours. Plus, we were tired. Pit's sister and wife also jumped in on a few of these laps and ran portions with us, which was a lot of fun.

On lap thirty of thirty-two, Pit said he wanted us to hold the Luxembourg flag as we ran in together. I encouraged him to go on without me, but he didn't want to speed up and seemed very content to finish together. Lap thirty-two was still fast but more of a celebratory lap as we both knew we'd finish it together. We came around the last corner and saw his wife holding the flag for us. We each grabbed a corner of the flag and ran through the finish line tape together. It was epic! 3:09:23 was our time.

After five marathons, here were the standings:

David: 1st place
Pit: 2nd place (two hours behind David)
Me: 3rd place (two minutes behind Pit)
Andrew: 4th place (about 20 minutes behind me)

While worship music was my choice in Dubai, this race brought out the country in me. I listened to Pat Green for the first twenty miles. Nothing makes me think of Natalie more than Pat Green music. Natalie mentioned him to me the first time we met, so he quickly became my favorite. Around mile eighteen, Pat Green's "Crazy" came on, and I sang most of it loudly during the loop and even through the main area where everyone was standing. I thought, "Who cares? I'm five marathons deep into the week. We're all going a little crazy! Man, I miss her!"

After the race, I talked with Pit's family for a bit but left them so they could enjoy each other. I found the showers and cleaned up, then Dave and I decided to walk back toward the town square and look for food. We found a small sidewalk restaurant.

They didn't speak any English, and neither of us speak much Spanish. We learned the only main course they had left was suckling lamb. It's risky to try a strange new food when your body is stressed from exercise and there's a stomach bug going around, but we decided to go for it.

The lamb was good enough, soaked in a broth with french fries that were also soaked in the broth. I drank a beer, and David had water (Yes, maybe that's another reason he's faster than me). Afterward, we found a small bakery, grabbed some sweets, and made our way back toward the sports complex to load the bus and head toward the airport.

A few hours pass, and it's now 11:00 p.m. Keep in mind ... we were supposed to run in Fortaleza, Brazil at 7:00 p.m., and it's a seven-and-a-half-hour flight, so we won't even arrive before 2:00 or 3:00 in the morning. There's really no way we get this done within the seven-day time limit, but none of us really care if it ends up being seven days plus four hours. We just want to finish strong. Plus, we want to finish together. We have forged some awesome friendships. When you push yourself to extremes with a group of like-minded people, it's hard to not grow close. Suffer together. Grow together. I walked a lap with Sally Orange tonight as she had her toughest race yet. She was emotionally spent, exhausted. We walked and jogged together, enjoying an opportunity to encourage one another. That's part of what this event is about. It's about spurring one another on, encouraging each other, loving your neighbor, and sharing God's love with random deeds. It's beautiful.

Today's Run:

European leg of the World Marathon Challenge 5, 26.03 miles at 7:16 pace in 3:09:23. Best race so far!

That's part of what this event is about. It's about spurring one another on, encouraging each other, loving your neighbor, and sharing God's love with random deeds. It's beautiful.

Michael and Kelly giving us a Spanish bullfight

Marathon 5 starting line in Torrelaguna, Spain

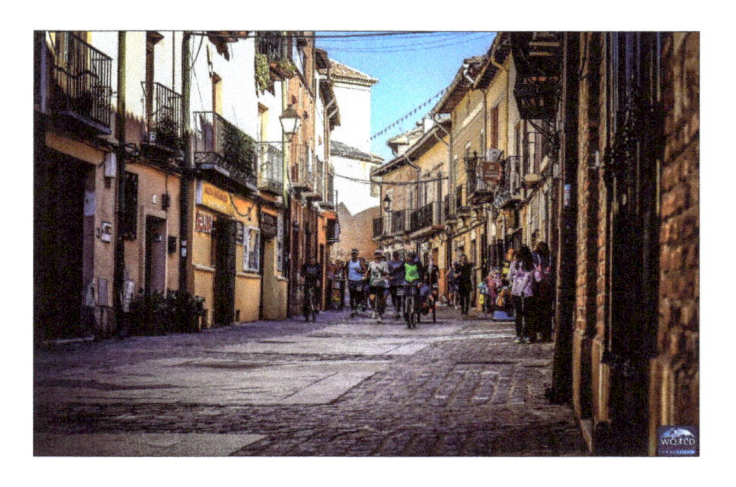

Start of the race running through a beautiful European town

Pit and Andrew on my right and left early on in Spain

European hills were brutal

Crossing the finish line holding the Luxembourg flag next to Pit and Laurence

Pit and I celebrating at the finish

Day 13:

Monday, February 6, 2023, Part 1 of 2
Fortaleza, Brazil.

It's 2:30 a.m., *and we are almost to Fortaleza. We "officially" have twenty-four hours to be completely done. Two marathons to go! This is supposed to be the hard one, the penultimate race in a tough climate, but I'm excited because I get to see my family tonight!*

> *"Lord, you formed the earth; help me enjoy your creation today, worship you, and remember you while running. Please give me an unknown supply of energy. Please help me continue to love others in such a way that they see Jesus in me and desire something I have. In Jesus's name, amen."*

Today has been crazy! We landed at 3:30 a.m. and were ready to run in Fortaleza on the northeastern Atlantic coast of Brazil. Of course, everyone changed clothes on the plane and was prepared. I slept in business class last night and had a pretty good night of rest. The flight from Madrid to Fortaleza is only seven and a half hours, so I probably only got about six hours of sleep.

We got off the plane with the intention of quickly going through customs and jumping on a bus to get to the race. As we got through customs, we waited for about thirty minutes before being told we needed to go back to the baggage area and get our bags as they offloaded them from the plane. This was not the plan. We thought we had checked our bags in Dubai all the way to Miami, but evidently, that wasn't the case, and they wouldn't let us keep them on the plane.

Richard told a few of the runners that once we got to the course, we would only have about four and a half hours to complete the marathon, so he suggested starting to get in mileage now. So, while we were in the airport waiting on bags, a number of runners started doing laps around the baggage carousel. People were walking and jogging around the small airport area, and many completed two, three, and four miles while waiting for luggage.

We waited almost ninety minutes for all of the bags to get off the plane! We had no idea what was going on. We grabbed our stuff and headed back through customs. As we gathered on the other side of customs, we were met by another Brazilian authority employee who told us it was all a mistake, and we really didn't need to grab our bags. Instead, he told us, "Leave everything sitting there in the airport." I'm not sure how everyone else felt, but leaving my bags in the middle of the airport lobby and walking away didn't seem smart. But we were running out of options. We all stacked our gear in a corner while frustration was mounting in all of us. We'd now been at the airport for about three hours, and the clock was ticking. We had just under twenty-one hours to run a marathon, then fly from Brazil to Miami to get to South Beach to run another marathon. The situation was looking more and more bleak. Our deadline was 12:22 a.m. Tuesday morning. We finally boarded the bus, and I'm certain we had the slowest bus driver in Brazilian history. We actually had two people on bicycles pass us on the way to the beach! What took us half an hour in a return drive later in the day took over an hour in the morning with no traffic.

We finally arrived. There was only one porta potty, and it was by far the nastiest I've ever been in. And I've done a lot of races. This one had blood-spattered napkins and what had to be at least week-old feces. It was horrendous. Fortaleza was not impressive.

As the sun was rising, we all lined up, and Richard quickly gave us instructions for a mile out and back loop course for thirteen total loops. The temps were in the mid-eighties, and the humidity was close to 90 percent. It was going to be tough, about as tough as having to endure that porta potty.

The race started with Dave in the lead, followed by Andrew, then me, with Pit following. This was only the second race that Pit and I didn't start together. I think everyone was so mixed up from the morning mess that we didn't even think about running together. It's like we were all off our game a little. We stayed in this order for the first sixteen miles, but I was fading fast. We all were, but I was fading more than the others. Pit passed me between miles sixteen and eighteen. We were still clipping off 7:50 paces, but it was getting miserable. The toll of the last six days was catching up to us.

The last eight miles were insane. Temps and humidity were both hovering around ninety. The course was packed with people all along Mucuripe Beach. People were playing Brazilian Beach soccer-volleyball, doing yoga, riding bikes, running, and much more. It was packed! I even ran a lap with some Brazilian runners, and that helped pass the time even more. They wanted to know all about the other days and couldn't believe what we were doing. We talked for at least three to five miles about the previous races. I powered through, but the pace continued to struggle. I finally started my thirteenth loop, dodged people on the pathway, and finished in fourth place with a time of 3:30:50. What is worse is that my watch showed I went 26.86 miles. I never mind going over the normal 26.2-mile distance, but that's over a half mile extra. That adds four minutes to your time on a nasty tough day.

My body was spent. My mind was spent. Spiritually, I was spent. I was completely zapped. But the end of the journey was near, and I had to keep pressing on.

After the race, Pit and David told me the first bus was leaving in thirty minutes, so I quickly rushed into a condo across the street for a shower. Some of my running clothes were so nasty from the humidity and sweat that I decided to leave them there. We arrived back at the airport, where more problems awaited us. As we checked in, the internet went out, and they couldn't figure out how to get us checked in. It took, on average, fifteen minutes per person to get through check in. Brazil was quickly becoming the worst part of my trip. I needed to remember what Richard told us originally. He was in charge, and we shouldn't worry. He would take care of it. For the first time during the past two weeks, I allowed the stress of the travel to get to me, and I needed to let it go. It was forcing me to exert energy that I didn't have the capacity to give.

I finally made it through check-in and met up with Andrew and Pit at the airport food court. I ordered a pizza and coke and started replenishing my energy.

I'm tired. "Lord, help me today. I have another race tonight, and not only are my legs trashed, but my mind is now spinning from the travel stress today. I'm hurting in lots of ways. I'm so worried we'll run in the middle of the night, and my family will be forced to stay up late. Lord, help. Give me peace of mind. Give me a double dose of rest, and please restrengthen my body to run one more race. Keep me healthy, I pray, and watch over me. Help my attitude glorify you and encourage others. Amen."

Today's Run:

26.86 miles for Marathon 6 of the World Marathon Challenge in 3:30:50 for a 7:51 average pace. Sufferfest!

The start of marathon 6 in Fortaleza, Brazil

Michael dressed up in Fortaleza

Dan Little, 80 years old, powering through the Brazilian humidity

Finishing in Brazil and just relieved it's over

Day 13:

Monday, February 6, 2023, Part 2 of 2
Fortaleza, Brazil to Miami, Florida USA

I woke up *on the plane, but the lights were still off. That's a first for this trip. The scripture that came to mind was Philippians 2:15–16: "So that you may become blameless and pure, 'children of God without fault in a warped and crooked generation.' Then you will shine among them like stars in the sky as you hold firmly to the word of life. And then I will be able to boast on the day of Christ that I did not run or labor in vain."*

I'm ready to get there. Ready to see Natalie. Ready to see my parents. Ready to see Matt and Lucy, our best friends. I can't wait! I'm also ready to run. My body is tired, but I have another marathon in me. It kinda makes me wonder how long I could keep doing this. I've gotten stronger this week.

If I could take this week and sum it up in one word, it's a word I'd take from the devotional my friend Mark wrote to me, and that word is "stronger." It stood out as soon as I read it, and my close friend and counselor, Randy, has told me that if something stands out like that, I should consider the Holy Spirit is probably trying to tell me something.

I believe the Holy Spirit is trying to tell me that I'm stronger because I have an inner strength that doesn't come from physical training but from the Holy Spirit living in me. As Zach mentioned in his devotional to me, training for holiness has a parallel connection to training for running. I am not my own; I was bought with the price of the cross. In his entry, Dustin encouraged me to keep my focus on the cross of Christ. When I look back over the devotionals my friends and family wrote, I can see how God has his hand in all of them.

I am stronger because of this week. I'm stronger for being able to put myself through this grueling ordeal. I'm stronger because I've spent time praying and meditating on my Lord. I'm stronger because I am his, and he is mine. I'm stronger for having spent a week with more than fifty amazing individuals who have pushed themselves beyond normal human limits. We've encouraged each other and supported each other for every step while we've also laughed together, cried together, hurt together, and celebrated together. I'm stronger because I miss my family. I'm stronger because I see what the world has to offer, and it's nothing compared to the riches I have in Christ. I'm stronger today than I was a week ago, and I'm grateful for this lesson.

"Lord, tonight, continue to be my strength. Help me not run in vain but shine like the stars. Amen."

Day 14:

Monday, February 6 – Tuesday, February 7, 2023
Miami, Florida, USA

We deboard the plane, and the Miami airport is laid out in such a way that we probably walked close to two miles from the plane through the airport to the waiting buses. Other than the airport layout, the Miami race and logistics were well organized. We loaded our bags on a U-Haul truck and jumped onto the bus. It still took time, but this was much more efficient than most of our other stops.

We loaded up and headed out from the airport. On the Fortaleza bus ride, I allowed myself to doze and get sleepy because it took so long. I decided to not allow that here. I wanted to be fully awake at the beginning of this race. There's nothing tomorrow, so I can push a little extra tonight. Who knows what the legs will have left in them, but knowing my family will be there is going to help.

I keep checking my travel app to see how far away we are from the beach. I can't wait to see Natalie! It's been two weeks. Finally, the bus stops, and we file off. I'm halfway back in the bus and looking through the windows, I'm trying to spot my *dad. He's always the easiest for me to find. I walk down the stairs, step out onto the street, and start walking through the crowds of families. People are hugging and loving on their husbands, wives, dads, moms, sisters, brothers, friends, and children who have just traveled the world to run marathons.*

Finally, I looked over and saw Natalie standing up on a curb to my left. Tears welled up in my eyes. My breath stopped. It had been so long since I had seen her. I missed her so much. Yes, distance can make the heart grow fonder. We hugged, kissed, and just spent a minute being with each other. It was perfect, and she was happy to hug me because I wasn't sweaty and nasty yet! My mom, dad, Matt, and Lucy were all there. We hugged, laughed, and enjoyed being with each other.

Saying I'm grateful they were there is a gross understatement. I looked forward to it all week! It's one of the hopes I had to look forward to, and it would help carry me forward.

We had about fifteen minutes to enjoy our families and loved ones. Now, it was time to race. I rushed over to a large bathroom area, but it was all locked up since it was almost midnight on South Beach. I walked over to the beach and did a "runners kneel" (where you act like you're tying your shoe but you're actually going pee pee) behind a wall. I jogged back over to the start, handed my gear to my dad, grabbed a few gels, and made my way to the start.

The atmosphere was the best of the week. It was almost midnight on Monday. So many family members were there from around the world. It was electric. Munish, Pit, and I did our quick picture at the starting (as we have done at each race). A few fist bumps were passed around to encourage each other, then Richard addressed us one last time as a group. He said, "One week ago, we were in Antarctica about to run a marathon. Since that time, you have been to seven continents and run six marathons. Let's do one more!" He told us this would be a 2.63 mile out and back for five loops of 5.25 miles each. He then moved out of the way and did one final countdown: "3, ... 2, ... 1, ... GO!"

We were off. I pushed through the crowd a little quicker this time and jumped up to the front, behind David, of course, within twenty feet or so of the start. I didn't want to dodge people for one hundred yards. Pit and Andrew were right with me.

Thinking back to the rankings, from my math, after Spain, Pit was two minutes ahead, but he added another three minutes in Brazil. Andrew was about twenty minutes behind me after Spain but beat me by five minutes in Brazil. So, he was fifteen minutes behind me overall. He ran a 2:36:00 marathon a few years back, so he definitely has the *speed to catch up. If he beats me by 15 minutes he would move into third place for the week, pushing me to fourth. For me to move into second place overall, I would need to beat Pit by five minutes. I only did that once this week in South Africa, so it is highly unlikely.*

We jumped into a fast pace early on, which had me a little worried. This was the third marathon in thirty-six hours and seventh in the week, but who cares, it's the last one. I don't need to run thinking about tomorrow anymore. I can leave it all out on the course tonight.

We ran miles one through six at 7:04, 6:57, 7:14, 7:08, 7:14, and 7:04. This was the fastest we'd gone all week. You could tell there was excitement and an edge of competition going on tonight. The course was flat, and although it was windy off the beach, there were plenty of plants and shrubs all along the course to block the winds, which made for a fast course. The temps hovered in the upper sixties to low seventies also, so it was one of the best running days of the week.

We ran north along Miami's South Beach. We passed nightclubs and restaurants, where food wasn't the only thing on the menu. More than once, we caught a whiff of marijuana so strong it almost knocked you off your feet. We got to the first turnaround point and ran back south toward the starting area. Natalie and my family were standing about fifty yards from the finish, and the closer we got, the more people there were to cheer us on. We saw the end of loop one and quickly grabbed a cup of water and headed back out for loop two.

David was easily out in front, but the three of us were flying as we went out for loop two. I kept doing the math in my head. If I could hang with Andrew at least to mile twelve, then he would be forced to run a minute per mile faster than me for the rest of the race to catch me for the entire week. I'm not sure if he even cared or knew the standings, but if he knew the numbers, and if I stayed close, it would break him mentally or physically. Every race this week except Antarctica, he has started out blazing fast but has faded some near the end. I needed to stay with him long enough that he knew I wasn't going away.

Pit looked strong. Early in this race, I conceded the overall weekly second place battle to him outside of the rare possibility he would fall apart later. I genuinely enjoyed seeing him race. He has become a close friend over the past two weeks, and if I have to lose the second-place battle to someone, there's no one else I'd rather it be.

We continued pushing through mile eight and reached the midway turnaround on the second lap.

Andrew was about ten steps back. Was he beginning to fade?

I took my first gel, grabbed some water, and kept moving. Gradually, I noticed fewer shadows around me and fewer feet hitting the ground. Andrew was fading. Now, I just needed to focus on staying the course. We were still running fast, but we were now running back to see family where they were stationed close to the start/finish area. Pit and I cruised into the loop two turn around to start loop three with Andrew now about a tenth of a mile behind us. My cousin Matt jumped in for about a quarter mile and asked how I was feeling. I told him I felt good which was actually true.

We kept pushing. And that's when it hit me. I caught a second wind and felt like I was flying. I believed I could run all night. This often happens during a race. I go through ups and downs and hope the ups last a lot longer than the downs. We made it to the midway turnaround again, and by now, Andrew was falling more than a half mile behind. It was over. The race for third overall was done. That was a relief. With only thirteen miles to go, I felt strong.

I told Pit around mile fifteen that we could finish this lap together, but then I'd let him go once we started lap four. We finished lap three and started lap four with an average pace around 7:15.

Despite me encouraging him to take off, we continued to run together until near the end of loop four, around mile twenty. Pit told me he was going to push for the final 10k, which was good with me. Running the last 6.2 miles of this epic journey alone sounded perfect. It would give me a little time to pray and reflect.

Lap five began. This was it, the end of the seven marathons. Ten out and backs in Antarctica, six loops in Africa, twenty-one loops in Australia, twelve loops in Asia, thirty-two loops in Europe, thirteen loops in South America, and now four out and backs done in North America with one more to go. I started out loop five and ran by my family with a little more than five miles to go.

I kept the pace between 7:20 and 7:36 for miles twenty-one to twenty-four and felt good. I picked it up for the last two, running mile 25 at a 7:13 pace and finishing mile twenty-six at a 6:52 clip, my last mile and fastest mile of the entire week. I came across the finish line in third at 3:11:18, my second-best time of the week at an average pace of 7:16. My wife and mom were holding the finish line tape, and my dad stood next to Richard, waiting for me to run through. It was epic.

Richard walked up, gave me a congratulatory hug, and placed three medals around my neck, one for finishing the North America Marathon and one for making my way into the Intercontinental Marathon Club, a feat of running a marathon on every continent. The last medal was a large one for finishing the World Marathon Challenge of 7 Marathons, on 7 Continents, in 7 Days.

David Kilgore and Pit Van Rijswick were standing there waiting for me, first, second, and third place for the week. We took time celebrating each other's accomplishments, taking photos, and congratulating one another. Then, I saw my family standing there waiting for me. I was completely nasty and sweaty, but I rushed over. My dad was the first one I got to. We hugged and just loved the moment. Next, I hugged my wife despite the fact that I was really gross. My mom hugged me because you're never too gross for your mom. Matt and Lucy hugged me too. Being runners, they understand the nastiness. It was magical. I've teared up plenty this week. The devotional book made me cry multiple times. Thinking back to family at different times did it too, but right now, there were no tears. It was simply exhaustion and joy. I was done. I was with my family, and it was perfect.

We hung around the finish line for a few hours, cheering on the other runners, celebrating each other's accomplishments, and enjoying the atmosphere one last time. We drank beer with many of the others and drank well into the morning hours.

Everything was coming to a close, and it was hard to let go. We finally left to try and rest around 5:30 a.m. on Tuesday morning. There were a few runners left on the course. Looking back, I regret leaving before everyone was done, but I also wanted to stay with my family, and they were ready to rest.

So, it was all finally done; years in the making and all done in one week. I ran 183.4 miles, visited seven continents, maintained an average marathon time of 3:25:43 (7:51 per mile), and had a total running time of twenty-three hours and fifty-six minutes. I had been on nine flights with seventy-six hours in the air from Dallas back to Miami, plus countless other hours in airports.

It was a tough week but wonderful in a million ways. The friendships will sadly fade, but the memories will last for decades. The life lessons will last even longer. I hope they'll last generations. Endurance matters. Whether it's running, marriage, kids, work, whatever—endurance matters, and even more so when you do it for the glory of God. As you endure, He will make you stronger if you stay focused

> Endurance matters. Whether it's running, marriage, kids, work, whatever—endurance matters, and even more so when you do it for the glory of God. As you endure, He will make you stronger if you stay focused on him and stay focused on the prize toward which He has called you.

on him and stay focused on the prize toward which He has called you. All of this can't be done well without community. Support and love are foundational to life. Love others and watch how they pour out so much love in return. We are not meant to do life alone. We are made to be in community with others.

> "Lord, I'm not even sure what to pray sometimes, so I'm grateful that your Holy Spirit intercedes on my behalf. Praise you, Lord. You formed the foundations of the earth. You created the winds in Antarctica. The snow and ice come and go as you desire. You created the rocky coastline of South Africa and the rugged mountains perched nearby. You formed the depths of the Indian Ocean, and with a touch of your finger, you dug it out like clay and placed a large island in the far corner. On that island are beautiful rivers and sunsets that only you could paint. God, you created the sands of the Middle East, the same sands which, thousands of years ago, your one and only son walked on, the same sand that he would eventually be laid to rest in, and the same sand that he would be resurrected from. Lord, you created the snowcapped Spanish mountains and

rolling foothills. You shaped South America as it juts out into the Atlantic Ocean. You created the thousands of people groups who call it home. And finally, Lord, you created my home in North America, lovely and beautiful, rugged and awesome. Lord, I sit here and contemplate the creation you let me see, and I am in awe.

> We are not meant to do life alone. We are made to be in community with others.

Lord, so many people back home have been following my journey. Thank you for giving me the endurance to finish this race for your glory and not my own. May this adventure be used as a light to draw people to you, I pray, amen."

Today's Run:

World Marathon Challenge Race 7 in Miami on South Beach. 26.33 miles in 3:11:18 at a 7:16 average pace. It is over. Let's do it again!

From left to right: My dad (Ken), my mom (Dietra), Matt, Lucy, and Natalie waiting for me to arrive in Miami

Munish, myself, and Pit pre-race in Miami

Miami starting line

Pit and I on lap 2

Starting my final lap in Miami

Finish line with my wife and mom holding the tape

Finish line with Richard

Pit after Miami Marathon

From left to right: Pit-2nd place; me-3rd place; David-1st place

Seven Days Later:
Waxahachie, Texas

The World Marathon Challenge is over. A week has gone by since I've returned home. I've enjoyed my two minutes of celebrity status. Okay, I'm not sure anything "running" gets celebrity status. Most people in this world have no idea who Eliud Kipchoge, the greatest marathoner of all time, is. He's the Michael Jordan and Tiger Woods of our sport! He'll run Boston this year, and if you're a runner, you won't want to miss it. So, my two minutes of fame have come and gone. And I'm grateful for that.

As we boarded the plane in Miami, I received a phone call from Universal Studios NBC, which is our channel 5 news team in Dallas. They asked to meet me for an interview and agreed to meet me at the baggage claim upon arrival. I walked through the baggage claim doors, and the camera was already pointed my way. Over the coming days, the NBC footage was shown in Dallas, Longview, Houston, other Texas markets and even into Arkansas. I received texts and emails from friends across the state. I also did a local sports radio show to talk about the adventure. I hosted a Q&A session at my church, and about 250 people attended.

Munish and Pit, as well as many of the other runners, are all going through the same in their hometowns. Pit was on a morning show in Luxembourg. Dierdre told her story on a podcast. Munish joined a radio show, and many others have been interviewed to tell their version of our adventure.

The Instagram and Facebook messages, texts, and other messages have calmed down now, and life is returning to normal. This makes me think, though: I keep telling people this was the trip of a lifetime. It was even life-changing in a thousand ways. Was it really? Is my life different? Is my outlook different? Will Pit and I remain friends for life? Will Munish come visit? What about Sally, Lauren, Kelly-Ann, Tuya, Kelly, Justin, BJ, Michael, David, Karan, Ben, Carter, and so many others? Was this only about running?

My spirit and my soul cries out, "NO! Don't let the lessons learned over the past week be lost in the blink of an eye." Friendships may come and go, and I hope to run into each of these wonderful friends along some trail in the future, but there's so much to take away from this experience.

#1 It's Not Just Mental.

I love the friends or acquaintances that come up to you after you've run a fifty-mile ultramarathon, or a 10k for that matter, and say, "Oh man, that's such a mental challenge." Yes, it is mentally challenging. You must push yourself mentally beyond the pain and struggle, but it's so much more than that. The mental challenge doesn't matter if the physical isn't ready.

Physically, I push my body beyond what most people are willing to do. I have a friend who works in the home office of the same company I work for. He's heavily into the CrossFit Games. He's become the Fittest Man in New York and Missouri for his age group. No doubt he's dedicated to his craft. He spends hours and hours every week perfecting what he does, watching what he eats, resting, and more to prepare physically for what he knows will be a mental grind.

Similarly, I put in miles after miles after miles. Some days are slow and easy (some runners call these junk miles). The idea is to add mileage on tired legs, and it's very important. Other days, I'm working on my anaerobic threshold and pushing my limits on the track, in a tempo run, fartleks, or some other speed workout. My diet is a struggle, but I focus on what I eat when a race is approaching. I sacrifice in other areas of life to rest or stretch appropriately so I can get up for a 4:00 a.m. run if necessary. All of this is physically demanding, and it's the physical strength that tells my mind I can do it.

Mentally, I'm ready because when I'm running a race, and the "wall" (that force that tells you there's no way you can take another step) hits me, I remember all of the days, hours, miles, sacrifice, struggle, and grit it took to get to where I am. When you have done all of this, then you can overcome the mental challenge. But it's the sacrifices along the way, the decisions you make, and the consistency throughout the process that prepares you for the mental battle.

#2 It Takes Discipline and Grit.

All of the lessons I learned are separate but inseparable. It's not just mental because it's a grueling test of physical endurance.

> It's the sacrifices along the way, the decisions you make, and the consistency throughout the process that prepares you for the mental battle

To prepare for this feat, it took a lot of discipline in my training to be prepared. There were days I woke up at 3:00 a.m. for a 3:45 run. I much prefer to run in the afternoon, even over the course of the summer months in Texas. Actually, I often ran in temperatures between 95–102 degrees. Every vacation, trip, and out-of-town experience always involves a training run. I took my family to Hawaii this past summer, and every day I got up early and went out for a run.

Running is fun for me most of the time, so it's not a burden. But there are plenty of days I just don't feel like it. Discipline is needed to make a commitment and stick to it. My family sacrifices as well. My wife understands the importance of training and allows me to schedule our calendar often around a training run or race.

It also takes grit. Every marathoner will tell you the race begins about mile twenty. Your body is breaking down, your heart rate is elevated, your legs start to give, and everything in you wants to stop. But you don't. You can't. Grit is that lever you pull that pushes you to keep going when others start walking. Grit is what it takes to sign up in the first place. Grit is what gets you to the finish line.

A lot of people read books, listen to podcasts, or follow David Goggins in one of his many outlets. David is an accomplished runner, inspirational speaker, and former Navy Seal. He thrives on pain and grit and toughness. Every speech is about not backing down. Before going out of town, Mark and Matt and I were on a training run talking about one of his latest Instagram posts. In the post, Goggins talks about how sometimes you feel beat up and want to quit. You feel all alone like you're stuck out in the middle of the ocean, and you begin to drown because you can't remember how to swim anymore, or your muscles just stop. At this point, Goggins looks straight at the camera and says, "You better learn how to f*%#ing backstroke." That's grit. We laughed about it as we ran, and more than once, we texted that quote to each other during my event.

#3 You Can Get Stronger.

As the week went along, my strength improved. Marathon number three in Australia scared me, yet I ran smart in Dubai, and by Madrid, I was ready to really push it. Physically, I was improving, and spiritually, I was also improving. Every day I had the chance to wake up, read my devotional, spend lots of time in prayer and focus on my Lord. Hurry is the great enemy of intimacy. On this trip, I couldn't hurry. I had to be patient. Go to the airport and wait. Get on the plane and wait. Finish a race and wait. I had plenty of time to focus on my God, which made me stronger. My faith became stronger, and the more time I spent praying, the more I wanted to spend. It was a wonderful getaway with the Maker of my soul.

Stronger. That's the word of the day and of the trip. I am

> Hurry is the great enemy of intimacy

stronger when my focus is on the prize, whether that be running, loving others, serving, or growing. "Hope will not disappoint us" when preceded by faith and perseverance through suffering. Instead, hope makes us stronger because "God's love has been poured out into our hearts through the Holy Spirit ... because Christ died for the ungodly" (paraphrased from Romans 5:3–6).

#4 It's Critical to Get Fully Away with Your God.

As I mentioned above, my spiritual relationship grew during this time. I went to run a group of races, yet what happened on this trip was so much deeper. I know how important it is to go on date nights with my wife. We love our two daughters, but if we don't spend time with just each other, we lose touch. In the same way, getting away and focusing on Jesus for a week made a difference. I had the chance to forget about work, volunteer needs, or community events. I even got to leave behind family obligations and focus on my relationship with my Lord. I learned it's critical to get fully away with my Lord on a regular basis. Maybe this means once a year for a week, or maybe it's once a month for an evening. That differs based on your season in life. God intended us to rest in him, to have a Sabbath rest, and this trip taught me the importance of making it happen.

#5 The World Doesn't Know Jesus, but They're Interested.

I didn't have a spiritual conversation with everyone on my trip, but I understand that faith was not a primary focus for many of them. One of the runners told me he'd read the Bible and loved the great lessons it shared. He also thought Jesus was amazing because of all of the wonderful things he did. That was it. Jesus was a good man, and he did great things. I wanted to cry out that Jesus is so much more! He's my Savior. He's the light of the world. He can save you too! Maybe it wasn't the right time. Maybe I was scared. I hope and pray my life, my actions, and my words during the week helped lead others toward Christ.

Another runner asked me about my tattoo, which is Hebrews 12:1–3 on the back of my leg. I shared a portion of the verse with them that you should "Throw off everything that hinders and the sin that so easily entangles. And let us run with perseverance the race marked out for us." She responded that this is a great verse to live by no matter what you believe. The Bible can change your world and your eternity if you give it a chance. Many people aren't anti-Christian. They just haven't been given the chance to meet the grace-giving, merciful, all-loving Jesus I know.

#6 Prayer Matters.

I don't know how many people were praying for me back home. But I do know I received prayers through texts and voicemails. Hundreds of people before, during, and after the event told me they were praying for me. People asked what they specifically needed to pray for, such as when I felt ill before Antarctica. Also, I dealt with bone spurs leading up to the WMC. Safe travels, time away from family, and so much more were prayed over.

I have not been in a situation, such as a sickness or death of someone in my immediate family, where I've asked for lots of people to pray, and because of that, I've never experienced the joy of feeling the power of prayer. This past week, though, I felt the power of prayer more than I can explain. I would ask for prayer about my anxious thoughts, and I would feel the Holy Spirit calm my anxiety. Others would pray for my illness or pray I didn't get the stomach bug, and each time I could feel God calm my nerves. I am definitely not saying that getting sick would have been God not answering prayers, but God chose to allow me to run healthy for some reason. He kept my body well, and I hope that allowed me to better love others, better run with endurance, and glorify him. If I had gotten sick, I hope that I would have praised God for allowing me to still be there, suffer, and endure in a different way, still to bring him glory.

#7 It Takes Community.

The Waxahachie Running Club and Midlothian Running Club communities are amazing. We run together, host races together, travel together, suffer and fight together, cheer each other on, battle each other, and have become so close in the process of it all. This community spurs me on to keep running and improving.

My church community supports me, loves me, prays for me, cares for my family, and pushes me to love others in everything I do. My work community also supports and helps me. The communities that God has surrounded me with continue to shape me into the man I am becoming. I meet with a group of men weekly to read through the Bible and encourage each other. These men push each other to love the Lord and serve the world around us.

During my time away, these communities reached out to me constantly. I received messages at all hours of the day encouraging me, inspiring me to keep going, and pushing me not just to run hard but to serve and love others in the process.

I also had the joy of community within the new set of friends I made on this trip. Watching an eighty-year-old gentleman push his body to complete all seven marathons inspired all of us. Seeing thirteen-year-old kids run 13.1 miles every day was amazing. Blisters, strained muscles, messed up knees, and so many other ailments would have stopped almost anyone in a normal race. But when you surround yourself with extraordinary people, you become extraordinary also. You cannot help but keep going when those around you won't let you stop.

#8 Endurance Is a Lifestyle.

I pray daily that the endurance I have built as a runner helps me endure the everyday struggles that come in marriage, parenthood, job issues, and more. Life is hard. It's that simple. Endurance is hard. Our world has a tendency to say it's okay to quit, to stop the suffering, or lessen your objective. There may be times when goals need to change, a marriage needs to end, or a different job is required, but if we are not careful, we can look for easier ways out of difficult times too often. We want the quick fix or the money-making scheme that requires no work.

Endurance is not a lottery. It takes blood, sweat, tears, and struggle. If I can learn to endure running mile after mile, I believe that's a lesson that can transform the rest of my life as well.

#9 Adventure Awaits.

Life is an adventure. I can't wait to see what's next in my racing schedule or in some cool getaway with my family. Pit, Munish, and I are thinking of getting together to race around Luxembourg. I'm not sure exactly what the calendar holds, but I'm certain God has something in store for all of us. Running the 777 was amazing, but being a dad is also an epic adventure! I'm a horrible dancer, but I'll be doing my kids' daddy-daughter dance on stage in front of hundreds of people come spring. I'll embarrass myself all day long if it makes my daughters' smile. Marriage is an adventure. Every day, Natalie and I learn new lessons about raising kids, loving each other, serving, sacrifice, and more. We travel the world together, but simply doing life together is the most amazing adventure ever.

The world is not enough. Nothing satisfies. No adventure, no journey, no race—nothing fully satisfies. Everything leaves

---

Endurance is not a lottery. It takes blood, sweat, tears, and struggle

---

you needing more, desiring a bigger adventure, a new challenge. As soon as one experience is over, I immediately need the next fix. It's fun for the moment, but it never lasts. And that's how God created each one of us. I've heard it said many times and have experienced it once again this week. Inside each person is a void only God can fill. We can live our entire life trying to fill it with something or someone, only to still be empty. It's a God-sized void that only he can fill.

I have found only one thing to quench that thirst, and that is Jesus Christ. I find satisfaction, joy, excitement, and adventure in my

> But when you surround yourself with extraordinary people, you become extraordinary also. You cannot help but keep going when those around you won't let you stop

relationship with him. I am not my own. Instead, I believe I was bought at a price. Jesus, the Son of God, sacrificed his life on a cross, was buried, and rose again so I could be forgiven of my sins, so I could live eternally in heaven with my Savior. I desire to honor God with my life. I desire to honor him in my running, my marriage, as a parent, and at work. If I keep finding races, then I pray that as I run, it will give me opportunities to share his love with others and bring glory to him. In turn, I pray that my passion spurs and inspires others to know him as I know him.

#10 Dare to Know Jesus.

If you can't find satisfaction, I dare you to try Jesus. If you have tried adventures, climbed mountains, run races, fought battles, built companies, and more seeking to live life to the fullest, yet you still have a void, then I dare you to try Jesus. Living your life with Jesus, being able to talk to the God of the universe, and listening to his Spirit guide you is an epic adventure.

For many years, I have also derived strength and wisdom from many authors and world-renowned leaders. Scott M. O'Neill wrote the book, "Be Where Your Feet Are." The whole premise of his book is to be present where you are. Put the phone down. Turn the TV off and seek adventure with your family. Go outside. Play in the rain. Get dirty. Go for a run!

Put the phone down. Turn the TV off and seek adventure with your family. Go outside. Play in the rain. Get dirty. Go for a run!

One of my favorite quotes is from Teddy Roosevelt, the twenty-sixth president of the United States. He penned the words,

It is not the critic who counts; not the man who points out how the strong man stumbles, or where the doer of deeds could have done better. The credit belongs to the man who is actually in the arena, whose face is marred by dust and sweat and blood; who strives valiantly; who errs, who comes short again and again, because there is no effort without error and shortcoming; but who does actually strive to do the deeds; who knows great enthusiasms, the great devotions; who spends himself in a worthy cause; who at the best knows in the end the triumph of high achievement, and who at the worst, if he fails, at least fails while daring greatly, so that his place shall never be with those cold and timid souls who neither know victory nor defeat.

And to sum it all up, one of my new favorite quotes comes from Dan Little, the eighty-year old gentleman who also completed seven marathons on seven continents in seven days. He was asked why he did this race. He paused briefly, smiled, and said, "It is the feeling of feeling half dead and never more alive at the same time."

And that, my friends, is my story of endurance. It is a story written by all who have given so much to me. It is a story that God allowed to be written. And it is a story I'm glad to have shared.

> "It is the feeling of feeling half dead and never more alive at the same time."

Celebration night with my family

The love of my life – Natalie

Acknowledgments

> *Do you not know that your bodies are temples of the Holy Spirit, who is in you, whom you have received from God? You are not your own; you were bought at a price. Therefore honor God with your bodies.* — 1 Corinthians 6:19–20

I thank God that he has given me the ability to run and the desire to do so for long distances. I hope and pray my running glorifies him and draws others to him.

I am so grateful for my wife Natalie. She is patient, kind, beautiful, loving, and beyond what I deserve. She supports my crazy habit, and I think she secretly even likes that I do it. There is no one I'd rather see at a finish line, and she is the only person I am seeking to impress.

Thank you to my daughters, Kenlee and Annie, who are my inspiration. As a dad, everything I do is for you. I can't tell you how many times your beautiful faces come to my mind in every race and inspire me to keep going.

Thank you to my parents, who are the least selfish people I know. They tirelessly serve and love with grace and humility. I want to be you when I grow up.

Thank you to my friend and past running partner Andrew White, who took many hours to read, edit, and correct countless grammatical errors in my journal. You spent Sunday afternoons with me pouring over the document, and I am grateful for your friendship and expertise. This never would have happened without your dedication and support.

Thank you to Candace Ahlfinger and Kirk Lewis, who took time to read, edit, and share ideas to help this book come to life. I was ready to simply be done until you gave me the hope that someone might actually enjoy reading it.

Thank you to Lauren Cavett, who also helped edit. Seeing this document from the eyes of another participant was invaluable. She inspires runners every day in Beaumont, Texas.

Thank you to so many running friends who have logged miles with me. Running is a community. Trails or roads, it doesn't matter. I just love being around other runners. Matt Gore, I'm not sure I would have ever actually signed up for my first marathon if you wouldn't have done so first. I love you, buddy, and am forever grateful God gave me you as a cousin. Matt Curtis, we have run countless races together (which I'm certain I've beaten you more than you've beaten me!). We have shared great times, hard times, pain, and joy, all while pounding the road. I am a better man having you to run beside. Mark Miller, the last few years have been awesome pushing each other since you are one of the most easily athletically gifted people I know. I've enjoyed every mile and every spiritual and not-so-spiritual conversation. WRC and MRC, I love you all and am grateful for a community that pushes each other to do more than what the mind could imagine.

I feel like I could write an entire book thanking people who have encouraged my running, but this definitely wouldn't have been possible without Richard Donovan and his entire team. Richard was an incredible race director, but more than that, he is a pioneer in the running world who is pushing boundaries to create stories and events that are shaping the world of running.

Lastly, thank you to my new WMC friends who I met in January 2023. We traveled the world, struggled through airports, cried, sweated, and bled together. I miss you and love you all. You inspire me and so many others. I am honored to have my name next to yours on the list of those who have run 7 Marathons in 7 Days on 7 Continents.

My last 13 weeks of Training Plan

10/31–11/6	57.15 total miles	8m @ 8:07 pace	8m @ 6:44 pace	weights	10m @ 8:21 pace
11/7–13	31.2 total miles	6m @ 8:08 pace + strides	rest/knee problems	rest/knee problems	8m @ 7:16 pace + weights
11/14–20	55.1 total miles	8.13m @ 8:15 pace	10m @ 7:27 pace	rest	6m @ 8:15 pace
11/21–27	60.25 total miles	6.05m @ 8:37 pace +weights	rest	8.2m @ 7:40 pace	10m @ 7:13 pace
11/28–12/4	62.1 total miles	5m @ 9:50 pace on trails	10m on trails @ 18:42 pace	weights	8m @ 8:00 pace
12/5–11	30.6 total miles	rest	6m @ 8:32 pace	8m @ 8:16 pace	6.1 @ 8:22 pace
12/12–18	65.2 total miles	rest	10m @ 7:39 pace	12m @ 7:41 pace	6m @ 8:35 pace + weights

continued:

8m on treadmill @ 8:01 pace	15m hillwork @ 7:47 pace	8.15 @ 8:27 pace + weights
2.10 @ 8:59 pace + weights	5m @ 7:01 pace	10.1m @ 8:33 pace
6m @ 7:47 pace + weights	10m @ 7:24 pace	15m @ 7:33 pace + weights
8m @ 7:34 pace + weights	12m @ 7:38 pace	16m @ 7:22 pace
8m @ 7:35 pace + weights	13.1 @ 7:34 pace	18m @ 7:50 pace
weights	5.5 @ 7:29 pace	5m @ 6:58 pace
6.4m @ 7:54 pace	12.6 @ 7:44 pace	18.2m @ 7:37 pace

12/ 19–25	70.2 total miles	6.1m @ 8:20 pace + weights	12m @ 7:45 pace	14m @ 7:29 pace
12/ 26–1/1	79.2 total miles	4.15m @ 8:24 pace	12m @ 7:57 pace	16m @ 7:46 pace
1/ 2–8	60.5 total miles	weights	8.2m @ 7:52 pace + weights	10.1m @ 7:36 pace
1/ 9–15	80.5 total miles	6.5m @ 7:10 pace	8m @ 7:49 pace + weights	6m @ 8:05 pace
1/ 16–22	52.7 total miles	6m @ 8:31 pace	6.3m @ 8:10 pace	8.1m @ 8:04 pace
1/ 23–29	28.8 total miles.	6.1m @ 8:25 pace	4m @ 6:50 pace + weights	6.5m @ 8:28 pace
1/30.	1.5m total before the marathons began.	1.5m COVID Test store run @ 7:26 pace		

weights	20m @ 7:55 pace	12m @ 7:29 pace	6m @ 8:20 pace
rest	3m @ 9:12 pace + 3m hiking w/family	18m @ 7:51 pace	22m @ 8:01 pace on trails + 1m cool down @ 14:02 pace
8m @ 8:03 pace	10m @ 7:48 pace	20m @ 7:42 pace	4.15m @ 8:31 pace + weights
4.2m @ 7:53 pace	0.6m warm up + 26.2 Unofficial Waxahachie Marathon in 3:21:24 @ 7:41 pace. Plus 0.6m shakeout later	0.8m warm up + 26.2 Unofficial Irving Marathon in 3:21:26 @ 7:41 pace.	1.4m shakeout @ 7:50 pace
weights	8.2m @ 7:38 pace	12m @ 7:47 pace	12m @ 7:37 pace
In flight	6m in Cape Town @ 7:42 pace	6.2m @ 8:03 pace finish w/Munish	Rest/ Penguin Day

Schedule I put together with my packing list the week before I left

Date	Place (of departure)	To (travel & arrival info)
January 25	Dallas	Qatar Airlines, DFW to Doha, QR732, 10:55 p.m., 14h25 flight
January 26	Doha, Qatar	Arrive Doha, 10:20 p.m.
January 27	Cape Town, South Africa, Winchester Mansions Hotel	Qatar Airlines, Doha to Cape Town, QR1369, 2:15 a.m. to 11:15 a.m., 10h0 flight
January 28	Cape Town, South Africa, Winchester Mansions Hotel	
January 29	Cape Town, South Africa, Winchester Mansions Hotel	
January 30	Cape Town, South Africa, Winchester Mansions Hotel	

continued:

Race Info (est. start times)	Est. Time on Ground	Clothes/ Cubes	Recovery & Carry-on
8 miles training, 7:45–8:15 pace, 4x strides		Travel attire plus travel 2nd day	Antarctica gear. Few extra clothes & toiletries
63–84 degrees, 6 easy shakeout miles, 7:45–8:15, 4x strides	Arrive		Jawku, stretch
6 easy miles, 7:45–8:15 pace, 4x strides	All day		Jawku, stretch
Rest, walk	All day		Jawku, stretch
10 min shakeout, 4x strides	All day		Jawku, stretch

January 31	Cape Town, South Africa, Winchester Mansions Hotel leave 9:00	Novo, Antarctica. Arrive 14:30. 5hr30 flight	ANTARCTICA. 16:00 start. 15–30 degrees, windy. 6 loop groomed run on ice/snow, flat, non-technical.
February 1	Novo, Antarctica, leave 00:30 to Cape Town, South Africa leave 22:00 to Perth	Cape Town, South Africa. Arrive 06:00. 5hr30 flight	AFRICA. 10:00 start. 63–84 degrees. 6 loops, flat.
February 2	in flight	Perth, Australia. Arrive 14:30. 10hr30 flight	AUSTRALIA. 18:00 start. 66–88 degrees. Night run, 8 loops, flat.

8hr30	Antarctica cube. Run tights, UA shirt, short sleeve shirt, Dallas Marathon half zip, rain jacket, beanie, mittens, glove liners, 2x socks, trail shoes, goggles, neck buff	Wear to & from Antarctica: uw, socks, tights, jeans, warm undershirt, long sleeve shirt, pullover, beanie, road run shoes, coat, hand/foot warmers
16hr00	Africa cube. Shorts, singlet, socks, road shoes	Still have hotel room to shower & clothes all in luggage.
18hr00	Australia cube. Shorts, singlet, socks, road shoes	West Australian Marathon Club, nice facilities, aid stations, etc. May stay overnight. Shorts, uw, socks, T-shirt, pullover, sandals

Endurance: 7 Marathons on 7 Continents in 7 Days | 169

February 3	Perth, Australia, leave 08:30	Dubai, United Arab Emirates. Arrive 16:50. 12hr20 flight	ASIA. 20:00 start. 60–90 degrees. Jumereih Beach, 10 loop course out & backs, rubbery path, soft on legs.
February 4	Dubai, UAE, leave 10:50	Madrid, Spain. Arrive 15:50. 8hr25 flight	EUROPE. 18:00 start. 37–53 degrees. Jarama Formula 1 racing track, rolling hills.
February 5	Madrid, Spain, leave 05:50	Fortaleza, Brazil. Arrive 10:15. 8hr25 flight	SOUTH AMERICA. 13:00 start. 77–88 degrees, Beach & park path, loops.
February 6	Fortaleza, Brazil, leave 02:15	Miami, USA. Arrive 08:05. 7hr50 flight	NORTH AMERICA. 11:00 start. 64–75 degrees. South Beach, loops
February 7	Miami, USA, Benley Hotel		
February 8	Miami, leave 10:00	Dallas, TX. AA2206. 10:00 to 12:25. 3hr30 flight	

18hr00	Asia cube. Shorts, singlet, socks, road shoes	Will have hotel room & sleep post-race. Shorts & pants, T-shirt, hoodie, uw, socks, sandals
14hr00	Europe cube. Shorts, gloves, hat, singlet, long-sleeve shirt & black zip-up, road shoes	Venue has showers, rest areas, etc. Shorts, pants, hoodie, T-shirt, uw, socks, sandals
16hr00	SA Cube. shorts, singlet, socks, road shoes	Shorts, pants, uw, socks, T-shirts, zip-up, sandals
24hr55	NA cube. Shorts, singlet, socks, road shoes	Bentley Hotel
All day		
Go home		

Endurance: 7 Marathons on 7 Continents in 7 Days

Every Race Cube	Medical Cube	Tech & Carry-On
sunglasses	Advil	converter
gels	Tylenol	all chargers!
Body glide	blister meds	journal, iPad, books
Vaseline	needle	headphones
sunscreen	scissors	passport
yoga mat	salt tabs	cash
K&A bracelets	Anti-nausea Rx & regular	neck pillow
race belt	sleep meds	pens, glasses
headlamp	lip balm	masks
4 calf sleeves	antibiotics	vaccination card
water bottle	steroids	daily meds
Jawku	butt-paste	AirPods
toiletries	Band-Aids	
Camp towel	muscle cream	

Other Clothes		Other Gear
2 run shorts	3–4 non T-shirts	freeze-dried meals
2 run shirts	2–3 run shoes	snacks
sandals	15 uw	peanut butter
travel shoes		toiletries w/razor, nails, clippers
2 run hats + 2 other hats		shampoo, shower gel
raincoat?		
2 travel sweatpants		
2–3 pants		
4 short sleeve T-shirts		
3 long sleeve T-shirts		
1 hoodie & 1 zip up		
2 shorts		
10 socks + 2 extra run socks		
Reuse Antarctica gear		